Lecture Notes in Economic
and Mathematical Systems

D1867368

31

Carlo Giannini

Topics in Structural VAR Econometrics

Springer-Verlag
Berlin Heidelberg New York
London Paris Tokyo
Hong Kong Barcelona
Budapest

Author

Prof. Carlo Giannini
Department of Economics
University of Ancona
Via Pizzecolli 68
I-60121 Ancona, Italy

ISBN 3-540-55262-6 Springer-Verlag Berlin Heidelberg New York
ISBN 0-387-55262-6 Springer-Verlag New York Berlin Heidelberg

Printed in Germany

Typesetting: Camera ready by author
Printing and binding: Druckhaus Beltz, Hemsbach/Bergstr.
42/3140-543210 - Printed on acid-free paper

To Vittoria and Andrea

CONTENTS

Foreword

In recent years a growing interest in the structural VAR approach (SVAR) has followed the path-breaking works by Blanchard and Watson (1986), Bernanke (1986) and Sims (1986), especially in U.S. applied macroeconometric literature.

The approach can be used in two different, partially overlapping directions: the interpretation of business cycle fluctuations of a small number of significant macroeconomic variables and the identification of the effects of different policies.

SVAR literature shows a common feature: the attempt at "organizing" - in a "structural" theoretical sense - instantaneous correlations between relevant variables. In non-structural VAR modelling, instead, correlations are normally hidden in the variance-covariance matrix of the innovations of VAR models.

Structural VAR analysis tries to isolate ("identify") a set of independent shocks by means of a number of meaningful theoretical restrictions. The shocks can be regarded as the ultimate source of stochastic variations of the vector of variables which, moreover, could be seen as potentially all endogenous.

Looking at the development of SVAR literature I felt that it still lacked a formal general framework which could embrace the several types of model so far proposed for identification and estimation.

Following Rothenberg (1971, 1973) the present monograph tries to develop a methodological framework for three types of model which encompass all the different models used in applied literature. I have also tried to generalise the identification and estimation set-up using the most general type of linear constraints available for the representation of ideas about the organisation of instantaneous co-movements of variables in response to "exogenous" independent shocks.

Trying to adapt recent work by Lütkepohl, section 5 contains calculations of the asymptotic distributions of impulse response functions and forecast error variance decompositions. This allowed me to avoid using bootstrapping or Monte Carlo integration techniques in the three types of model. Paragraph 5.b of this section was written by Antonio Lanzarotti.

Section 6, introductory in nature, includes some suggestions and warnings that may be useful in the treatment of deterministic components, typically long run constraints in a stationary context and a way to match a cointegrating set-up.

Section 7 tries to offer deeper insights into Structural VAR modelling. It contains very few technicalities and qualitatively discusses the results of an exercise carried out on Italian data using an AB-model. The exercise draws upon the economic framework put forward by O.J. Blanchard in its 1989 paper.

Annex 1 deals with the notion of structure in SVAR modelling, while Annex 2 contains my point of view on the significance of the three types of model discussed in this monograph. I also try to suggest some criteria on which model to choose in different applications together with some general considerations on their overall working.

Appendix A briefly summarizes rules and conventions of matrix differential calculus adopted in this monograph.

Appendix B contains the calculation of the first order conditions for the maximization of the likelihood of the "Key" model and the corresponding Hessian matrix.

Appendices C and D have been written jointly by Antonio Lanzarotti and Mario Seghelini: the former contains some examples of symbolic identification analysis for the K, C and AB models; the latter contains two RATS programs that implement the ideas put forward in this monograph.

Looking at a selected choice of recent SVAR applied papers one can see the following correspondence with regard to the categorization put forward in this monograph: O.J. Blanchard, M.W. Watson, 1986 (K-model); O.J. Blanchard, D. Quah, 1989 and M. Shapiro, M.W. Watson, 1988 (C-model); B. Bernanke 1986 and O.J. Blanchard 1989 (AB-model).

When I started to write the first draft of this monograph, no available work covered the full range of methods and issues used in VAR econometric literature. Since then, Lütkepohl's 1991 book entitled "Introduction to Multiple Time Series Analysis" has filled the gap. It now enables me, to my great relief, to avoid discussing the problems of vector autoregressive modelling and usual structuralization through Cholesky decompositions.

This monograph surely overlooks a number of important topics in SVAR modelling, the most important of which is probably how to choose between alternative structuralizations of the same unstructured VAR model. Although the issue could be treated as a problem of testing non-nested hypotheses, I believe that a recent paper by Pollack and Wales (1991) on the likelihood dominance criterion offers the most straightforward solution.

A first version of this monograph has already had a limited circulation as "Topics in Structural VAR Econometrics", *Quaderni di ricerca* of the Department of Economics of Ancona University, July 1991. I have since added Section 7, Annex 2 and made some minor changes in other sections. The present version is still to be regarded as something in between a first draft and a final version; comments and suggestions are therefore warmly welcomed.

In preparing this monograph I have been supported by a M.U.R.S.T. 40% research grant at Ancona University labelled "Modelli macroeconomici e analisi econometrica dinamica".

I wish to thank G. Amisano, S. Yadav and R. Mosconi for helpful discussions and M. Faliva for providing useful algebraic references while I was working on the first version. I am also indebted to S. Calliari, J.D. Hamilton, M. Lippi, J.R. Magnus, H. Neudecker, R. Orsi, P.C.B. Phillips, D.S.G. Pollock, H.-E. Reimers and to the unknown Springer referee for their suggestions and/or encouragement after reading the first version. Thanks are also due to Ubaldo Stecconi of Cooperativa Logos, Ancona, who revised the English manuscript and managed the typesetting.

Special thanks are due to my students at Pavia University Antonio Lanzarotti and Mario Seghelini both for their contribution and suggestions. They have accompanied me through a journey which had started in a fog of confused ideas.

The usual claims obviously apply.

Ancona, January 1992

Carlo Giannini
Dipartimento di Economia
Università di Ancona
Via Pizzecolli 68
60121 Ancona, Italy

1. Introduction

In order to introduce the basic elements of Structural VAR Analysis, let us suppose that we can represent a set of n economic variables using a vector (a column vector) y_t of stochastic processes, jointly covariance stationary without any deterministic part and possessing a finite order (p) autoregressive representation.

$$A(L)\, y_t = \varepsilon_t$$

$$A(L) = I - A_1 L - \ldots - A_p L^p$$

The roots of the equation $\det(A(L)) = 0$ are outside the unit circle in the complex domain and ε_t has an independent multivariate normal distribution with [0] mean.

$$\varepsilon_t \sim I\, MN([0], \Sigma)$$

$$E(\varepsilon_t) = [0]$$

$$E(\varepsilon_t \varepsilon'_t) = \Sigma \qquad \det(\Sigma) \neq 0$$

$$E(\varepsilon_t \varepsilon'_s) = [0] \qquad s \neq t$$

(in other words ε_t is a normally distributed vector white noise)

The y_t process has a dual Vector Moving Average representation (Wold representation)

$$y_t = C(L)\varepsilon_t$$

$$C(L) = A(L)^{-1}$$

$$C(L) = I + C_1 L + C_2 L^2 + \ldots$$

where $C(L)$ is a matrix polynomial which can be of infinite order and for which we assume that the multivariate invertibility conditions hold, i.e. $\det(C(L)) = 0$ has all roots outside the unit circle, so

$$C(L)^{-1} = A(L)$$

From a sampling point of view, let us suppose we have T+p observations for each variable represented in the y_t vector; we are thus capable of studying the system

$$A(L)\, y_t = \varepsilon_t \qquad\qquad t = 1, \ldots ,T$$

This system can be conceived as a particular reduced form (in which all variables can be viewed as endogenous).

In order to relate our discussion to the usual Simultaneous Equations Systems formulae, this latest system can be re-written in compact form as follows (in relation to more usual Structural Systems Formulae we are assuming a "transposed" notation):

$$Y = A_1 Y_{-1} + A_2 Y_{-2} + \ldots + A_p Y_{-p} + V$$

or even more compactly

$$Y = \Pi\, X + V$$

where

$Y = [y_1, y_2, \ldots, y_T]$ — Y has dimension $(n{\times}T)$

$Y_{-i} = [y_{1-i}, y_{2-i}, \ldots, y_{T-i}]$ — Y_{-i} has dimension $(n{\times}T)$

$V = [\varepsilon_1, \varepsilon_2, \ldots, \varepsilon_T]$ — V has dimension $(n{\times}T)$

$\Pi = [A_1, A_2, \ldots, A_p]$ — Π has dimension $[n{\times}(n{\cdot}p)]$

$X = [Y'_{-1} \mid Y'_{-2} \mid \ldots \mid Y'_{-p}]\,'$ — X has dimension $[(n{\cdot}p){\times}T)]$

If no restrictions are put on the Π matrix, the formulae for asymptotic least-squares estimation and maximum likelihood estimation of Π, say $\hat{\Pi}$, coincide:

$$\hat{\Pi} = Y X'(X X')^{-1}$$

Notice that on the basis of this formula the estimator $\hat{\Pi}$ is independent of the variance-covariance matrix of the error terms ε_t.

Under the hypothesis that the elements of y_t are stationary, we can assume that

$$\underset{T\to\infty}{plim}\ \frac{X X'}{T} = Q$$

where Q is a positive definite matrix.

Under the hypothesis introduced it can be easily shown that

$$\sqrt{T}(vec\hat{\Pi} - vec\Pi) \xrightarrow{d} N\left[[0], \Sigma_\Pi\right]$$

where the symbol *vecA* shall indicate, as usual, the column vector obtained by stacking the elements of the *A* matrix column after column, $\xrightarrow{d}$ means convergence in distribution (hereafter we shall employ usual asymptotic notations contained, for example, in White (1984) and Serfling (1980)) and

$$\Sigma_\Pi = Q^{-1} \otimes \Sigma$$

If no restrictions are imposed on the Σ matrix, its maximum likelihood estimate will be

$$\hat{\Sigma} = \sum_{t=1}^{T} \frac{\hat{\varepsilon}_t \hat{\varepsilon}'_t}{T}$$

where $\hat{\varepsilon}_t = y_t - \hat{A}_1 y_{t-1} - \ldots - \hat{A}_p y_{t-p}$, or more compactly

$$\hat{\Sigma} = \frac{\hat{V}\hat{V}'}{T}$$

where $\hat{V} = Y - \hat{\Pi}X$.

A consistent estimate of Σ_Π is given by:

$$\hat{\Sigma}_\Pi = T \cdot (X X')^{-1} \otimes \hat{\Sigma}$$

Recent literature on the so-called Structural VAR Approach uses different ways of structurizing the VAR model. We will discuss three such ways: a <u>KEY</u> model which we will call the K-model, the C-model and the AB-model.

In addition to the hypotheses we introduced earlier, for the K-model (<u>KEY</u> model) the following expressions will hold:

K-model

K is a $(n \times n)$ invertible matrix

$$K\,A(L)\,y_t = K\,\varepsilon_t$$

$$K\,\varepsilon_t = e_t$$

$$E(e_t\,e'_t) = I_n$$

The K matrix "premultiplies" the autoregressive representation and induces a transformation on the ε_t disturbances by generating a vector (e_t) of orthonormalized disturbances (its covariance matrix is not only diagonal but also equal to the unit matrix I_n).

Note that assuming to know the true variance covariance matrix of the ε_t terms from

$$K\,\varepsilon_t = e_t$$

$$K\,\varepsilon_t\,\varepsilon'_t\,K' = e_t\,e'_t$$

taking expectations, one can immediately obtain

$$K\,\Sigma\,K' = I_n.$$

The previous equation implicitly imposes $n(n+1)/2$ non-linear restrictions on the K matrix leaving $n(n-1)/2$ free parameters in K.

C-model

C is a $(n \times n)$ invertible matrix

$$A(L)\,y_t = \varepsilon_t$$

$$\varepsilon_t = C\,e_t$$

$$E(e_t) = [0] \qquad\qquad E(e_t\,e'_t) = I_n$$

Sims (1988) stresses the point that there is no theoretical reason to suppose that C should be a square matrix of the same order as K. If C were a square matrix, the number of independent (orthonormal) transformed disturbances would equal the number of equations. Many reasons lead us to think that the true number of originally independent shocks to our system could be very large. In that case, the C matrix would be a $n \times m$

matrix with m much greater than n. In a sense, this research path is opposite to the one studied by the factor analysis, which attempts to find m (the number of independent factors) strictly smaller than n. The case of a rectangular $(n \times m), m > n$ C matrix conceals a number of problems connected with the completeness of the model and the aggregation over agents - see a short and not very illuminating discussion of this topic in Blanchard and Quah (1989).

In the sequel, we will not face this problem and will assume C square and invertible. Nevertheless, we think that many important issues can be better treated following the research path indicated here.

Turning back to our C model, the ε_t vector is regarded as being generated by a linear combination of independent (orthonormal) disturbances to which we will refer hereafter as e_t. This may have a different meaning as regards the K-model.

As for the K-model, notice that from

$$\varepsilon_t = C\, e_t$$

$$\varepsilon_t\, \varepsilon'_t = C\, e_t\, e'_t\, C'$$

taking expectations,

$$\Sigma = C\, C'.$$

If, again, we assume to know Σ, the previous matrix equation implicitly imposes a set of $^{n(n+1)}/_2$ non-linear restrictions on the C matrix, leaving $^{n(n-1)}/_2$ free elements in C.

AB-model

A, B are $(n \times n)$ invertible matrices[1].

$$A\, A(L)\, y_t = A\, \varepsilon_t$$

$$A\, \varepsilon_t = B\, e_t$$

$$E(e_t) = [0] \qquad\qquad E(e_t\, e'_t) = I_n$$

---

1 The same argument discussed earlier on the size of matrix C also applies to matrix B.

The A matrix induces a transformation on the ε_t disturbances vector, generating a new vector ($A\,\varepsilon_t$) that can be conceived as being generated by a linear combination (through the B matrix) of n independent (orthonormal) disturbances, which we will refer to as e_t (obviously, this might have a different meaning as regards the models K and C).

As in the previous case from

$$A\,\varepsilon_t = B\,e_t$$

$$A\,(\varepsilon_t\,\varepsilon'_t)\,A' = B\,(e_t\,e'_t)\,B'$$

$$A\,\Sigma\,A' = B\,B'$$

for Σ known, this equation always imposes a set of $n(n+1)/2$ non-linear restrictions on the parameters of the A and B matrices, leaving overall $2n^2 - n(n+1)/2$ free elements.

Following Sims (1986) and supposing that there are no cross restrictions on Π and Σ, or better that there are no restrictions at all on Π while a set of restrictions are imposed on Σ, the identification and the F.I.M.L. estimation of the parameters of models K, C and AB could be based on the analysis of the following log-likelihood function

$$\mathcal{L} = c - \frac{T}{2}\log|\Sigma| - \frac{T}{2}\,tr(\Sigma^{-1}\hat{\Sigma})$$

From this function three different log-likelihood functions can be obtained for models K, C and AB by direct substitution of Σ:

K-model

$$\mathcal{L}(K) = c + T\log|K| - \frac{T}{2}\,tr(K'\,K\,\hat{\Sigma})$$

remembering that, from $K\,\Sigma\,K' = I$, and taking into account the invertibility of K, we can write

$$\Sigma = K^{-1}\,K'^{-1} = (K'\,K)^{-1}$$

$$\Sigma^{-1} = K'\,K$$

and by virtue of the fact that $\log|(K'\,K)^{-1}| = -\log|K'\,K| = -2\log|K|$;

C-model

$$\mathcal{L}(C) = c - T\log|C| - \frac{T}{2}\, tr(C'^{-1}\, C^{-1}\, \hat{\Sigma})$$

remembering that

$$\Sigma = C\, C'$$

$$\Sigma^{-1} = (\, C\, C'\,)^{-1} = C'^{-1}\, C^{-1}$$

and that

$$\log|C\, C'| = 2\log|C|;$$

AB-model

$$\mathcal{L}(AB) = c + T\log|A| - T\log|B| - \frac{T}{2}\, tr(A'B'^{-1}\, B^{-1}\, A\, \hat{\Sigma}),$$

remembering that

$$A\, \Sigma\, A' = B\, B'$$

$$\Sigma = A^{-1}\, B\, B'\, A'^{-1}$$

$$\Sigma^{-1} = A'\, B'^{-1}\, B^{-1}\, A$$

and that $\log|A^{-1}\, B\, B'\, A'^{-1}| = -2\log|A| + 2\log|B|$.

Looking at the three log-likelihood functions obtained by introducing the respective series of non-linear constraints on matrices K, C, A, and B, we can heuristically understand, that lacking further information, estimators for the parameters in K, C and A and B cannot be found.

All the sampling information is contained in $\hat{\Sigma}$ where, with probability one we have $n(n+1)/2$ distinct elements. By substituting Σ with the respective expressions of the different models we have overcome the problem of finding a direct estimate of the $n(n+1)/2$ different elements in Σ (which in reality was not known). The problem still remains of estimating

n^2 parameters for the K matrix in the K-model, n^2 parameters for the C matrix in the C-model and $2n^2$ parameters (n^2 for A and n^2 for B) in the AB-model.

It can be heuristically understood that from the knowledge (the sampling knowledge) of $\hat{\Sigma}$ a maximum of $n(n+1)/2$ functionally independent parameters for the three models respectively can be estimated. Without additional information we find ourselves in a typical situation of under-identification.

In general, Structural VAR Analysis has confined its attention to cases where, through exclusion restrictions, we can reach the exact identification of the whole set of parameters. One remarkable exception is a RATS routine, written by Doan in three different versions (1987, 1988, 1989). Doan proposes a complete solution for the estimation of over-identified and exactly identified models of the AB type with B diagonal and exclusion restrictions on the off-diagonal elements of the A matrix.

The exclusion restrictions and the need for exact identification greatly reduce the practical meaning of the Structural VAR Approach for a number of reasons - which shall be discussed below. To the best of my knowledge, still in the case of exact identification, two papers have tried to introduce new features. In the first paper, Blanchard and Quah (1989), the C-model is used for n=2 and the exact identification is obtained by introducing a homogeneous restriction on the parameters of the C matrix through an infinite-horizon theoretical constraint. In Keating (1990), instead, the AB-model is used for n=3 with B diagonal and a set of non-linear restrictions on the off-diagonal elements of the A matrix. These restrictions are derived from a variant of Taylor's rational expectations model.

In what follows we have tried to solve the problem of identification, estimation and use of K, C and AB models with additional linear restrictions of the most general type in a general way, namely:

$$R_k \, vec \, K = d_k \qquad \text{for K-model}$$

$$R_c \, vec \, C = d_c \qquad \text{for C-model}$$

$$\begin{cases} R_a \, vec \, A = d_a \\ R_b \, vec \, B = d_b \end{cases} \qquad \text{for AB-model}$$

where the R_i matrices ($i = k, c, a, b$) are matrices of full row rank.

To these groups of non homogeneous linear restrictions written in implicit form correspond three groups of restrictions written in explicit form - see for example Sargan (1988):

$$vec\,K = S_k\,\gamma_k + s_k$$

$$vec\,C = S_c\,\gamma_c + s_c$$

$$\begin{cases} vec\,A = S_a\,\gamma_a + s_a \\ vec\,B = S_b\,\gamma_b + s_b \end{cases}$$

where the S_i, $(i = k, c, a, b)$ are full column rank matrices and the number of columns is equal to the number of free elements in the respective matrices.

The number of rows of the S_i matrices is obviously n^2 and the number of columns is n^2 minus the number of rows of the corresponding R_i matrix.

The following identities will hold for the R_i, d_i, S_i and s_i vectors and matrices

$$R_i\,S_i = [0] \qquad [0] \text{ is a matrix of appropriate order}$$

$$R_i\,s_i = d_i \qquad i = k, c, a, b$$

Following the terminology of Magnus (1988), when $d_i = [0]$, $i = k, c, a, b$, the K, C, A, B matrices are called L-structures (*linear* structures); whereas when $d_i \neq [0]$ they are called *affine* structures.

2. Identification Analysis and F.I.M.L. Estimation for the K-Model

The K-model[1] is completely defined by the following equations and distributional assumptions:

$$K\,\varepsilon_t = e_t$$

$$E(e_t) = [0] \qquad E(e_t e'_t) = I_n$$

$$\varepsilon_t \sim I\,MN\,([0], \Sigma) \qquad det(\Sigma) \neq 0$$

(ε_t, the vector of the VAR model disturbances $A(L)\,y_t = \varepsilon_t$, is a Gaussian vector white noise, i.e. a vector of independent multivariate normally distributed variables with an associated positive definite variance-covariance matrix).

All the sampling information is contained in the $\hat{\Sigma}$ matrix:

$$\hat{\Sigma} = \frac{\hat{V}\hat{V}'}{T}$$

The $\hat{\Sigma}$ matrix can be viewed as the unrestricted estimate of the variance-covariance matrix of the disturbances of the "reduced form":

$$A(L)\,y_t = \varepsilon_t$$

The corresponding log-likelihood function of the K-model for the parameters of interest (the n^2 parameters in the K matrix) is

$$\mathcal{L}(K) = c + T\log|K| - \frac{T}{2}\,tr(K'\,K\,\hat{\Sigma}) \tag{1}$$

---

1 Hereafter we will drop the i index ($i = k, c, a, b$) to R_i, d_i, γ_i, S_i, s_i matrices and vectors unless ambiguity arises.

With respect to this function, the associated density function and the "structural" parameter space, we will assume that all the usual regularity conditions hold - as quoted in Rothenberg's (1971) fundamental paper on identification.

The conditions

$$K \Sigma K' = I_n$$

obviously introduce a set of non-linear restrictions on the parameter space. Therefore, in general, we can obtain only necessary and sufficient conditions for local identification of the parameters in the K matrix as opposed to *global* identification (See Rothenberg (1971), p. 578.).

Moreover, we are interested only in the joint identification of all K matrix parameters (in the sense of Wegge (1965), we are interested in the identification criteria of a system of equations as a whole) and not in the "isolated" identification of a proper subset of parameters of the K matrix. In Structural VAR Econometrics all the equations of a structuralized VAR are used together, thus "isolated" identification of a proper subset of the parameters in question is practically of no interest.

In order to achieve identification we will assume that the parameters contained in the K matrix will satisfy the set of independent, non-contradictory, non-homogeneous linear restrictions stated in implicit form as follows

$$R \, vec \, K = d \tag{2}$$

where R is a $r \times n^2$ full row rank matrix and d is a possibly non zero $r \times 1$ vector, or in explicit form

$$vec \, K = S \gamma + s \tag{3}$$

where S is a $n^2 \times l$ full column rank matrix with $l = n^2 - r$, s is a $n^2 \times 1$ vector and

$$\underset{r \times l}{R S = [0]}$$

$$\underset{r \times 1}{R s = d.}$$

Following Rothenberg (1971), in order to geometrically analyze the local non-identification situation in the absence of a-priori information contained in (2) or (3), we will compute the information matrix (the sample information matrix) of the vectorized elements of the *K* matrix, without taking into account the set of linear restrictions (2) or (3).

For this purpose we shall compute the vector of partial first derivatives of the log-likelihood function with respect to *vecK* (the "score" vector) and then the Hessian matrix of the log-likelihood (always with respect to *vecK*). From this last expression we can now easily compute the sample information matrix.

Taking into account the symbols and notations presented in Appendix A, the score of the likelihood function is (see Appendix B for calculation)[2]

$$\frac{\partial L}{\partial\, vec\, K} = f'(vec\, K) \qquad f'(vec\, K) \text{ is a } 1\times n^2 \text{ row vector}$$

$$f'(vec\, K) = T\,(K^{-1})^{r} - T(vec\, K)'\,(\hat{\Sigma} \otimes I)$$

or equivalently (see Pollock 1979), taking into account that

$$(A)^{r} = [vec\,(A')]'$$

$$f'(vec\, K) = T\left[vec(K')^{-1}\right]' - T(vec\, K)'\,(\hat{\Sigma} \otimes I);$$

obviously the first order conditions for maximization of the likelihood function are

$$\underset{(1\times n^2)}{f'(vec\, K)} = \underset{(1\times n^2)}{[0]}$$

in row form, or

$$\underset{(n^2\times 1)}{[f'(vec\, K)]'} = \underset{(n^2\times 1)}{f(vec\, K)} = \underset{(n^2\times 1)}{[0]}$$

---

2 In order to simplify notation, the I_n identity ($n\times n$) matrix will hereafter be substituted simply by I. Identity matrices of different orders will be indicated with their proper corresponding index.

in column form.

Again referring to Appendix A for notation rules and to Appendix B for calculation, the Hessian matrix of the log-likelihood with respect to *vecK* is defined as

$$\frac{\partial^2 \mathcal{L}}{(\partial\, vec\, K)\, (\partial\, vec\, K)'} = \frac{\partial}{\partial\, vec\, K}\left(\frac{\partial\, \mathcal{L}}{\partial\, vec\, K}\right)'.$$

The resulting Hessian can be written as

$$H\,(vec\,K) = \frac{\partial^2 \mathcal{L}}{\partial(vec\,K)\;\partial(vec\,K)'} = -\,T\left\{(K^{-1} \otimes K'^{-1})\, \textcircled{T} + \hat{\Sigma} \otimes I\right\}.$$

The sample information matrix of the elements of *vecK* (without taking into account the set of linear restrictions on this vector) has two equivalent definitions for "regular" likelihood functions

$$I_T\,(vec\,K) = E\,[-\,H\,(vec\,K)] \qquad (*)$$

$$I_T\,(vec\,K) = E\,[f\,(vec\,K) \cdot f'\,(vec\,K)] \qquad (**)$$

Following (*) and taking into account that

$$E\,(\hat{\Sigma}) = (K'\,K)^{-1} = K^{-1}\,(K')^{-1}$$

$$I_T\,(vec\,K) = T\left\{\left[K^{-1} \otimes (K')^{-1}\right] \textcircled{T} + \left[K^{-1}\,(K')^{-1}\right] \otimes I\right\}$$

and the properties of the commutation matrix $\textcircled{T}$ (see Pollock 1979 and Magnus 1988) for A, B square matrices of order n

$$(A \otimes B)\textcircled{T} = \textcircled{T}(B \otimes A)$$

we can write

$$I_T\,(vec\,K) = T\left\{(K^{-1} \otimes I)\, \textcircled{T}\, (K'^{\,-1} \otimes I) + (K^{-1} \otimes I)\,(K'^{\,-1} \otimes I)\right\}$$

and finally

$$I_T\,(vec\,K) = T\left\{(K^{-1} \otimes I)\,(I_{n^2} + \textcircled{T})\,(K'^{\,-1} \otimes I)\right\}$$

The corresponding asymptotic information matrix

$$I\,(vec\,K) = \underset{T \to +\infty}{plim} \frac{1}{T} I_T\,(vec\,K)$$

will simply be:

$$I\,(vec\,K) = \{(K^{-1} \otimes I)\,(I_{n^2} + Ⓣ)\,(K'^{-1} \otimes I)\}.$$

The sample information matrix and the asymptotic information matrix are of $n^2 \times n^2$ order; it is easily seen however that in our case these matrices are singular, their rank being equal to $n(n+1)/2$.

Since $(K^{-1} \otimes I)$ and $(K'^{-1} \otimes I)$ are invertible matrices, the rank of $I_T\,(vecK)$ and $I\,(vecK)$ is equal to the rank of

$$I_{n^2} + Ⓣ$$

Using Magnus' (1988) notation and results[3] we define:

$$N_n = \frac{1}{2}\,(I_{n^2} + Ⓣ)$$

obviously[4] $r\,(N_n) = r(I_{n^2} + Ⓣ)$, but N_n is an idempotent matrix[5] with rank $n(n+1)/2$.

Assuming that the "true" value of the vector of parameters $vec(K_0)$ is a regular point of the information matrix $I_T\,(vecK)$ (in the sense of definition 4 of Rothenberg 1971, p. 579), and on the basis of Theorem 1 in Rothenberg (1971) which states as necessary and sufficient condition for the local identification of $vec(K_0)$ the non-singularity of

$$I_T\,(vec\,K_0)$$

we can assert, in view of the singularity of

$$I_T\,(vec\,K)$$

---

3 See Magnus (1988) p.48. In our notation the Ⓣ matrix replaces Magnus's K_{nn} commutation matrix.

4 As usual, $r(A)$ stands for the rank of matrix A.

5 From the property of the Ⓣ matrix, $Ⓣ \cdot Ⓣ = I_{n^2}$.

over all the (admissible) parameter space, that $vec(K_0)$ is unidentifiable.

In order to get necessary and sufficient conditions for the local identification of the complete vector $vecK$, we must re-introduce our a-priori information contained in

$$R\, vec\, K = d$$

which has thus far been overlooked.

Following Rothenberg (1971) and taking into account that, since the last set of constraints is linear, the Jacobian matrix of the partial derivatives of the system of constraints with respect to $vecK$ is simply R, we can construct the following matrix

$$V_T\,(vec\,K) = \begin{bmatrix} I_T\,(vec\,K) \\ R \end{bmatrix}$$

or equivalently

$$V\,(vec\,K) = \begin{bmatrix} I\,(vec\,K) \\ R \end{bmatrix}$$

These two matrices are of $(n^2 + r) \times n^2$ order.

Following Theorem 2 in Rothenberg (1971) and assuming that the "true" vector $vec\,(K_0)$ is a regular point (in the sense of Rothenberg) of $V_T\,(vec\,K)$ and $V\,(vec\,K)$, a necessary and sufficient condition for the local identification of $vec(K_0)$ is that the rank of $V_T\,(vec\,K)$ or $V\,(vec\,K)$ evaluated at K_0 be n^2.

In other words, the V_T (or V) matrices evaluated at $vec\,K_0$ must be full column rank matrices.

This necessary and sufficient condition is very difficult to verify in our context. We will then try to attain more tractable conditions which are still absolutely equivalent to those of Rothenberg's Theorem 2 [6].

Looking at $V\,(vecK)$ "augmented" matrix

---

6 In our context $I_T(vec\,K)$, $I\,(vec\,K)$ are matrices of constant rank $n(n+1)/2$ over the admissible parameter space (looking at the information matrix, the admissible space is also constrained by the invertibility of the K matrix). We can heuristically find a necessary condition for identification: taking into account the rank of matrix $I\,(vec\,K)$, one necessary condition is that it be "augmented" by at

$$V(vec\,K) = \begin{bmatrix} (K^{-1} \otimes I)\, 2N_n\, (K'^{-1} \otimes I) \\ R \end{bmatrix}$$

we can proceed as follows:

the rank of $V(vecK)$ is left unchanged if we premultiply and postmultiply this matrix by arbitrary non-singular matrices, obviously of the appropriate order.

If $V(vecK)$ is first premultiplied by the block-diagonal matrix

$$\frac{1}{2}\begin{bmatrix} (K \otimes I) & [0] \\ [0] & 2\,I_r \end{bmatrix}$$

and then postmultiplied by

$$(K' \otimes I)$$

the following $(n^2 + r) \times n^2$ matrix is obtained

$$\begin{bmatrix} N_n \\ R\,(K' \otimes I) \end{bmatrix}$$

Under the condition that $K' \otimes I$ is an invertible matrix (i.e. that K must always be an invertible matrix), this matrix is of the same rank as V_T and V.

The condition of full column rank (n^2) of this matrix is equivalent to the condition that the following homogeneous system of $(n^2 + r)$ equations in (n^2) unknowns

$$\begin{bmatrix} N_n \\ R\,(K' \otimes I) \end{bmatrix} y = [0]$$

has only one admissible solution $\underset{n^2 \times 1}{y = [0]}$.

This system can be split into two connected systems of equations

$$N_n\, y = [0] \qquad (4)$$

---

least $n(n-1)/2$ independent rows. In other words, a necessary condition for identification reads as follows: r, i.e. the number of restrictions over $vec\,K$, must be greater than or equal to $n(n-1)/2$.

$$R\,(K'\otimes I)\,y = [0] \qquad (5)$$

System (4) has n^2 equations in n^2 unknowns. System (5) has r equations in n^2 unknowns. The two systems are connected because they share the same n^2 unknowns.

In order to find closed formulae for the identification analysis we can now proceed in two ways: i) the general solution of system (4) is found and inserted in system (5) or ii) the general solution of system (5) is found and inserted in system (4).

The former procedure will be followed. The alternative has the advantage to lead to more "parsimonious" conditions for identification, which, however, are more difficult to interpret.

Considering system (4) and looking for the general solution of this system of equations we will follow Magnus (1988).

The vector representing the general solution of system (4) can be represented by

$$y = \tilde{D}_n x$$

where the $\tilde{D}_n$ matrix, defined in Magnus (1988), pp. 94-5, is a full column rank matrix of $n^2 \times n(n-1)/2$ order and x is a $n(n-1)/2$ vector of free elements.

The $\tilde{D}_n$ matrix's characteristic is that for every vector x (with real components) it generates the vectorized form of a skew-symmetric matrix (say $\underset{n\times n}{W}$, $W = -W'$) of order n.

$$y = vec\,W = \tilde{D}_n x.$$

We can easily check that this is a solution of system (4) remembering the property of the commutation matrix Ⓣ

$$Ⓣ\, vec\,A = vec\,A' \qquad \text{for } A(n\times n)$$

and that for a skew-symmetric matrix

$$vec\,W = -\,vec\,W'$$

so for

$$N_n = \frac{1}{2}(I_{n^2} + Ⓣ)$$

$$N_n \tilde{D}_n x = N_n \, vec\, W = \frac{1}{2}(I_{n^2} + Ⓣ)\, vec\, W = \frac{1}{2}(vec\, W + Ⓣ\, vec\, W)$$

$$= \frac{1}{2}(vec\, W + vec\, W') = \frac{1}{2}(vec\, W - vec\, W) = [0]$$

This solution is also the general solution by virtue of theorem 9.1 of Magnus (1988), p. 146. Having found the general solution of system (4), we can insert it in system (5), arriving at

$$R\,(K' \otimes I)\,\tilde{D}_n x = [0] \qquad (6)$$

Assuming the invertibility of the K matrix, the necessary and sufficient condition for identification of the "true" vector $vec(K_0)$ [7] can be wholly derived from system (6) and can be stated in two equivalent forms:

a)<u>Condition for identification</u>

Assuming the invertibility of the K matrix, the true vector $vec(K_0)$ is locally identified if, and only if, the matrix

$$R\,(K' \otimes I)\,\tilde{D}_n$$

evaluated at K_0 has full column rank $n(n-1)/2$

b)<u>Condition for identification</u>

Assuming the invertibility of the K matrix the "true" vector $vec\,(K_0)$ is locally identified if, and only if, the system

$$R\,(K' \otimes I)\,\tilde{D}_n x = [0]$$

with the matrix $R\,(K' \otimes I)\,\tilde{D}_n$ evaluated at K_0, has the unique admissible solution $x = [0]$.

In practical applications, condition a) can be used and numerically checked remembering to use

$$vecK = S\,\gamma + s$$

---

7 Obviously, the "true" vector $vec\,(K_0)$ must satisfy the constraints $R\; vecK = d$.

and assigning "random" numbers to the elements of the γ vector in order to insert a "proper" matrix in the $(K' \otimes I)$ nucleus of the formula.

The numerical check of the condition does not contribute much to understanding the role and working of different typical constraints.

In appendix C condition b) is used for the rather tedious symbolic analysis of a number of interesting cases.

Having assured the local identification of our vector of parameters, we can now move on to the estimation stage. In this context, it can be easily conducted using F.I.M.L. techniques; the natural algorithm on which we can concentrate is represented by the "score algorithm".

In order to avoid using Lagrange multipliers, the restrictions

$$R\, vec\, K = d$$

will be used in the connected explicit form

$$vecK = S\,\gamma + s.$$

Using the chain rule of differentiation we can look at the score vector for the free elements contained in the γ vector:

$$f'(\gamma) = \frac{\partial\, \mathcal{L}}{\partial\, vec\, K}\frac{\partial\, vec\, K}{\partial\, \gamma} = \frac{\partial\, \mathcal{L}}{\partial\, vec\, K} \cdot S$$

$$f'(\gamma) = f'(vec\, K)\, S = \frac{\partial\, \mathcal{L}(\gamma)}{\partial\, \gamma}.$$

The first order condition for the maximization of the log-likelihood with respect to γ are:

$$f'(vec\, K)\, S = \underset{1 \times l}{[0]}$$

in row form, or

$$f(\gamma) = S' f(vecK) = \underset{l \times 1}{[0]}$$

in "column" form. Taking into account that

$$vecK = S\,\gamma + s$$

is an affine function of γ we can use Theorem 11 by Magnus and Neudecker (1988, p.112) in order to find the Hessian matrix of γ

$$\frac{\partial^2 L(\gamma)}{\partial \gamma \partial \gamma'} = S' H(vec\,K)\,S$$

This expression clearly indicates that the sample information matrix of the parameter vector γ is simply

$$I_T(\gamma) = S' I_T(vec\,K)\,S$$

and the corresponding asymptotic information matrix is

$$I(\gamma) = S' I(vec\,K)\,S.$$

One can easily understand that the two latter matrices are invertible whenever the identifiability conditions are satisfied. The information matrix $I_T(\gamma)$ and the score vector $f(\gamma)$ can be used to implement the "score algorithm" and find a F.I.M.L. estimator of vector γ (say $\tilde{\gamma}$). Once the vector is obtained, we can get the F.I.M.L. estimator of $vec\,K$ (say $vec\,\tilde{K}$) using

$$vec\tilde{K} = S\,\tilde{\gamma} + s$$

The scoring algorithm for γ is based on the following updating formula (see for example Harvey (1990) p. 134):

$$\gamma_{n+1} = \gamma_n + \left[I_T(\gamma_n)\right]^{-1} f(\gamma_n).$$

Choosing the starting recursion values with great care, we can assume a consistent estimate ($\tilde{\gamma}$) of the "true" γ value (γ_0) can be obtained.

Inserting this value in the information matrix we can immediately get the estimated asymptotic variance covariance matrix of $\tilde{\gamma}$

$$A\hat{v}ar\sqrt{T}(\tilde{\gamma} - \gamma) = I(\tilde{\gamma})^{-1} = \left[\underset{T\to\infty}{plim}\frac{1}{T} I_T(\tilde{\gamma})\right]^{-1}$$

From this matrix we can get the estimated asymptotic variance covariance matrix of $vec\,\tilde{K}$ through the Cramer linear transformation theorem (see for example Theorem 4, Sargan (1988), p. 5):

$$A\hat{v}ar[\sqrt{T}(vec\,\tilde{K} - vecK)] = S\,I(\tilde{\gamma})^{-1}\,S';$$

under the hypothesis introduced, we obviously obtain

$$\tilde{\gamma} \sim A\,N\left[\gamma, \frac{1}{T}I(\gamma)^{-1}\right]$$

and

$$vec\,\tilde{K} \sim A\,N\left\{vecK, \left[\frac{1}{T}\cdot S\,I(\gamma)^{-1}\,S'\right]\right\}$$

Having obtained the F.I.M.L. estimate of *vec K*, $vec\,\tilde{K}$, we can reorganize it in matrix form getting the F.I.M.L. estimate of K (say $\tilde{K}$). From this matrix and taking into account the expression

$$\Sigma = (K'K)^{-1}$$

we can get the F.I.M.L. estimate of the (possibly) restricted variance covariance matrix of reduced form disturbances, ε_t

$$A(L)\,y_t = \varepsilon_t$$

through

$$\tilde{\Sigma} = (\tilde{K}'\tilde{K})^{-1}$$

In the case of over-identification, this matrix will not be equal to $\hat{\Sigma}$. Looking at the log-likelihood function

$$\mathcal{L} = c - \frac{T}{2}\log|\Sigma| - \frac{T}{2}\,tr\,(\Sigma^{-1}\,\hat{\Sigma})$$

and replacing Σ with $\hat{\Sigma}$ and $\tilde{\Sigma}$ where appropriate, we can easily construct a test of over-identifying restrictions

$$LR = 2\,\mathcal{L}(\hat{\Sigma}) - 2\,\mathcal{L}(\tilde{\Sigma})$$

This statistic under H_0 (the hypothesis of validity of the full set of identifying restrictions) is χ^2 distributed with a number of degrees of freedom equal to the number of over-identifying restrictions; looking at Appendix C, great care should be used to find the "true" number of over-identifying restrictions.

3. Identification Analysis and F.I.M.L. Estimation for the C-Model

The C-model is completely defined by the following equations and distributional assumptions:

$\varepsilon_t = C\, e_t$ C square of order n.

$E(e_t) = [0]$ $E(e_t e'_t) = I_n$

$\varepsilon_t \sim I\,MN\,([0], \Sigma)$ $det\, \Sigma \neq 0$

All the sample information is contained in the $\hat{\Sigma}$ matrix

$$\hat{\Sigma} = \frac{\hat{V}\hat{V}'}{T}$$

where, again, the $\hat{\Sigma}$ matrix can be viewed as the unrestricted estimate of the variance covariance matrix of the disturbances of the reduced form

$A(L)\, y_t = \varepsilon_t$

The corresponding log-likelihood function of the C-model for the parameters of interest (the n^2 parameters in the C matrix) is

$$\mathcal{L}(C) = c - T \log|C| - \frac{T}{2} tr\, (C'^{-1}\, C^{-1}\, \hat{\Sigma}) \tag{1}$$

This log-likelihood function can be written as follows

$$\mathcal{L}(C) = c + T \log|K| - \frac{T}{2} tr\, (K'\, K\, \hat{\Sigma}) \tag{1.b}$$

with $K = C^{-1}$.

We assume that all the usual regularity conditions (see Rothenberg 1971) hold for this function, the associated density function and the "structural" parameter space.

The conditions $\Sigma = C\,C'$ introduce a set of non-linear restrictions on the parameter space, therefore, in general, we can obtain only necessary and sufficient conditions for the local identification of the parameters in the C matrix (as opposed to global identification).

In order to achieve identification, we will assume that the parameters contained in the C matrix will satisfy the following set of independent non-contradictory, non-homogeneous linear restrictions stated in implicit form as

$$R_c \; vec\, C = d_c \tag{2}$$

where R_c is a $r\times n^2$ full row rank matrix and d_c is a possibly non-zero $r\times 1$ vector. In explicit form we have

$$vec\, C = S_c\, \gamma_c + s_c \tag{3}$$

where S is a $n^2\times l$ full column rank matrix with $l = n^2 - r$, and s_c is a $n^2\times 1$ vector, and

$$\underset{r\times l}{R_c\, S_c = [0]}$$

$$\underset{r\times 1}{R_c\, s_c = d_c.}$$

In order to geometrically analyze the local non identification situation in absence of the a-priori information contained in system (2), we will compute the information matrix of the vectorized elements of the C matrix, without taking into account the set of linear restrictions (2) or (3).

Using the chain rule of matrix differentiation and the two equivalent definitions of the information matrix

$$I_T\,(vec\, C) = -\,E\,[H\,(vec\, C)] = E\,[f(vec\, C)\cdot f'(vec\, C)]$$

we can bypass the direct calculation of the Hessian matrix with respect to $vecC$ on the basis of the following considerations.

The score vector of the log-likelihood with respect to $vecC$ can be obtained from the score vector of the log-likelihood with respect to $vecK$ on the basis of the following formula

$$\frac{\partial\, \mathcal{L}(C)}{\partial\, vec\, C} = \frac{\partial\, \mathcal{L}(C)}{\partial\, vec\, K}\,\frac{\partial\, vec\, K}{\partial\, vec\, C}$$

In fact, remembering that $C = K^{-1}$, $K = C^{-1}$ we can write

$$\frac{\partial \mathcal{L}(C)}{\partial\, vec\, C} = f'\,(vec\, K) \cdot \frac{\partial\, vec\, K}{\partial\, vec\, C}$$

with

$$\frac{\partial\, vec\, K}{\partial\, vec\, C} = -\left(C'^{-1} \otimes C^{-1}\right)$$

Therefore we have

$$\frac{\partial \mathcal{L}(C)}{\partial\, vecC} = -f'\,(vecK) \cdot \left(C'^{-1} \otimes C^{-1}\right)$$

But the following relationships also hold

$$I_T\,(vecC) = E\,[f(vecC) \cdot f'(vecC)]$$

$$I_T\,(vecC) = \left(C^{-1} \otimes C'^{-1}\right) E\,[f(vecK) \cdot f'(vecK)]\,\left(C'^{-1} \otimes C^{-1}\right)$$

$$I_T\,(vecC) = \left(C^{-1} \otimes C'^{-1}\right) I_T(vecK)\,\left(C'^{-1} \otimes C^{-1}\right)$$

Remembering the $I_T\,(vec\,K)$ formula and that $C = K^{-1}$, it can be shown that

$$I_T(vecC) = \left(C^{-1} \otimes C'^{-1}\right)\left\{T\,(K^{-1} \otimes I)\,(I_{n^2} + Ⓣ)\;\;(K'^{-1} \otimes I)\right\}\left(C'^{-1} \otimes C^{-1}\right)$$

$$I_T(vecC) = T\,[(I \otimes C'^{-1})\,(I_{n^2} + Ⓣ)\,(I \otimes C^{-1})]$$

$$I\,(vecC) = \underset{T \to \infty}{plim} \frac{1}{T} I_T\,(vecC)$$

$$I\,(vecC) = (I \otimes C'^{-1})\,(I_{n^2} + Ⓣ)\,(I \otimes C^{-1})$$

The sample information matrix $I_T\,(vec\,C)$ and the asymptotic information matrix are of $n^2 \times n^2$ order but it is easy to see that up to this point these matrices are singular, their rank being equal to $n(n+1)/2$.

Since $(I \otimes C'^{-1})$ and $(I \otimes C^{-1})$ are invertible matrices the rank of $I_T\,(vec\,C)$ and $I\,(vec\,C)$ is equal to the rank of

$$I_{n^2} + Ⓣ$$

and equal to the rank of

$$N_n = \frac{1}{2}(I_{n^2} + \textcircled{T}).$$

We assume that the "true" value of the vector of parameters ($vec\ C_0$) is a regular point of the information matrix $I_T(vec\ C)$, in the sense of Definition 4 in Rothenberg (1971). Theorem 1 in that same paper indicates the non-singularity of $I_T(vec\ C_0)$ as the necessary and sufficient condition for the local identification of C_0. Since $I_T(vec\ C_0)$ is singular, then $vec\ C_0$ is clearly unidentified.

Introducing the constraints

$$R_c\ vecC = d_c$$

and taking into account that, given the linearity of this set of constraints on $vecC$, the Jacobian matrix of the system of constraints is simply R_c; following Rothenberg (1971) we can construct the partitioned matrix

$$V_T(vec\ C) = \begin{bmatrix} I_T(vecC) \\ R_c \end{bmatrix}$$

or, equivalently, the matrix

$$V(vec\ C) = \begin{bmatrix} I(vecC) \\ R_c \end{bmatrix}$$

These two matrices are of $(n^2 + r) \times n^2$ order.

Following Theorem 2 in Rothenberg (1971), assuming that the "true" vector $vec\ C_0$ is a regular point (in the sense of Rothenberg's Definition 4) of $V_T(vec\ C_0)$ and $V(vec\ C)$, a necessary and sufficient condition for the local identification of $vec\ C_0$ is that the rank of $V_T(vec\ C)$ or $V(vec\ C)$ matrices evaluated at C_0 be n^2.

In other words, the V_T or V matrices evaluated at C_0 must be of full column rank.

In order to find more tractable conditions, we shall operate on the "augmented" $V(vec\ C)$ matrix, exactly as we have done for the K-model.

Let us look at the $V(vec\ C)$ "augmented" matrix:

$$V(vec\ C) = \begin{bmatrix} (I \otimes C'^{-1})\ 2N_n\ (I \otimes C^{-1}) \\ R_c \end{bmatrix}$$

It can be first premultiplied by the block-diagonal matrix

$$\frac{1}{2}\begin{bmatrix} (I \otimes C') & [0] \\ [0] & 2\, I_r \end{bmatrix}$$

and then postmultiplied by

$$(I \otimes C)$$

arriving at the following $(n^2 + r) \times n^2$ matrix

$$\begin{bmatrix} N_n \\ R_c\ (I \otimes C) \end{bmatrix}$$

which has obviously the same rank as the $V_T\ (vec\ C)$ or $V\ (vec\ C)$ matrices.

Following the same argument used for the K-model we can look at the system

$$\begin{bmatrix} N_n \\ R_c\ (I \otimes C) \end{bmatrix} y = [0]$$

trying to discover under which conditions it has the only admissible solution $y = [0]$.

The system can be split in two connected systems of equations:

$$N_n\, y = [0] \tag{4}$$

$$R_c\ (I \otimes C)\, y = [0] \tag{5}$$

Still by virtue of Theorem 9.1 in Magnus (1988), the general solution of system (4) is

$$y = \tilde{D}_n\, x$$

This (general) solution inserted in system (5) leads to

$$R_c\ (I \otimes C)\ \tilde{D}_n\, x = [0]. \tag{6}$$

Assuming the invertibility of the C matrix, the necessary and sufficient condition for identification of the "true" value[1] $vec\ (C_0)$ can be derived looking solely at system (6) and can be stated in these two equivalent forms:

a)<u>Condition for identification</u>: assuming the invertibility of the C matrix, the "true" vector $vec\ (C_0)$ is locally identified if and only if the matrix

$$R_c\ (I \otimes C)\ \tilde{D}_n$$

evaluated at C_0 has full column rank $n(n-1)/2$

b)<u>Condition for identification</u>: assuming the invertibility of the C matrix, the "true" vector vec(C_0) is locally identified if and only if system

$$R_c\ (I \otimes C)\ \tilde{D}_n\, x = [0]$$

with the matrix $R_c\ (I \otimes C)\ \tilde{D}_n$ evaluated at C_0, has the unique admissible solution $x = [0]$.

In practical applications condition a) can be used and checked numerically remembering to use

$$vecC = S_c\, \gamma_c + s_c$$

and assigning "random" numbers to the elements of the γ_c vector in order to insert a "proper" matrix in the $(I \otimes C)$ nucleus of the formula.

The numerical check of the condition does not contribute much to understanding the role and working of different typical constraints.

In appendix C, using condition b), we will propose a symbolic analysis of some interesting cases.

Having assured the local identification of our vector of parameters, we can now move on to the phase of its F.I.M.L. estimation. Still trying to avoid using Lagrange multipliers technique, we will use the following restrictions expressed in explicit form

$$vecC = S_c\, \gamma_c + s_c$$

---

1 Obviously, the "true" vector vec(C_0) must satisfy the constraints $R_c\ vec\ C = d_c$ in implicit form or $vec\ C = S_c\, \gamma_c + s_c$ in explicit form.

using the chain rule of differentiation we can find the score vector for the vector of the "free" elements γ_c:

$$f'(\gamma_c) = \frac{\partial L}{\partial\, vecK} \frac{\partial\, vecK}{\partial\, vecC} \cdot \frac{\partial\, vecC}{\partial\, \gamma_c} =$$

$$= -f'(vec\, K)\left(C'^{-1} \otimes C^{-1}\right) S_c = f'(vec\, C)\, S_c$$

The first order condition for the maximization of the log-likelihood with respect to γ_c are:

$$f'(\gamma_c) = f'(vec\, C)\, S_c = \underset{1\times l}{[0]}$$

in row form, or

$$f(\gamma_c) = S_c'\, f(vec\, C) = \underset{l\times 1}{[0]}$$

in column form.

Taking into account that

$$I_T(\gamma_c) = E\left[f(\gamma_c) \cdot f'(\gamma_c)\right] = S_c'\, [f(vecC) \cdot f'(vecC)]\, S_c,$$

we obtain

$$I_T(\gamma_c) = S_c'\left[I_T\, vecC\right] S_c$$

and obviously

$$I(\gamma_c) = \underset{T\to\infty}{plim} \frac{1}{T} I_T\,(\gamma_c) = S_c'\,[I\, vecC]\, S_c.$$

Using the information matrix $I_T(\gamma_c)$ and the score vector $f(\gamma_c)$ we can implement the score algorithm in order to find a F.I.M.L. estimator of γ_c (say $\tilde{\gamma}_c$) using the following updating formula:

$$(\gamma_c)_{n+1} = (\gamma_c)_n + \left[I_T\,(\gamma_c)_n\right]^{-1} f(\gamma_c)_n$$

At the end of the recursion, once $\tilde{\gamma}$ has been obtained, we can immediately obtain the F.I.M.L. estimate of vec C, say vec $\tilde{C}$, using

$$vec\tilde{C} = S_c\, \tilde{\gamma}_c + s_c$$

By inserting the $\tilde{\gamma}_c$ value in the information matrix we can immediately get the estimated asymptotic variance covariance matrix of $\tilde{\gamma}_c$:

$$A\hat{v}ar[\sqrt{T}(\tilde{\gamma}-\gamma)] = I(\tilde{\gamma}_c)^{-1} = \left[\underset{T\to\infty}{plim} \frac{1}{T} I_T(\tilde{\gamma}_c)\right]^{-1}$$

and from this matrix through the Cramer linear transformation theorem we conclude

$$A\hat{v}ar[\sqrt{T}\,(vec\tilde{C} - vecC)] = S_c\, I(\tilde{\gamma}_c)^{-1}\, S_c'.$$

Again $vec\tilde{C}$ is asymptotically normal distributed as

$$vec\tilde{C} \sim A\,N\left[vecC, \frac{1}{T} S_c\, I(\gamma)^{-1} S_c'\right]$$

Once we have obtained $vec(\tilde{C})$ we can reorganize this vector in matrix form arriving at $\tilde{C}$ (the F.I.M.L. estimator of matrix C). From this matrix, taking into account the expression

$$\Sigma = C\,C'$$

we can arrive at the F.I.M.L. estimate of the (possibly) restricted variance covariance matrix of reduced form disturbances, ε_t,

$$A(L)y_t = \varepsilon_t$$

through

$$\tilde{\Sigma} = \tilde{C}\,\tilde{C}'.$$

In the case of over-identification this matrix will not be equal to the unrestricted estimate of Σ, $\hat{\Sigma}$.

Again looking at the log-likelihood function

$$\mathcal{L} = c - \frac{T}{2}\log|\Sigma| - \frac{T}{2}\, tr(\Sigma^{-1}\hat{\Sigma})$$

and replacing Σ with $\tilde{\Sigma}$ and $\hat{\Sigma}$ where appropriate, we can easily construct a test of over-identifying restrictions

$$LR = 2\,\mathcal{L}(\hat{\Sigma}) - 2\,\mathcal{L}(\tilde{\Sigma}).$$

This statistics under H_0 (the hypothesis of validity of the full set of identifying restrictions) is χ^2 distributed with a number of degrees of freedom equal to the number of over-identifying restrictions, where great care must be used in order to find the true number of over-identifying restrictions.

4. Identification Analysis and F.I.M.L. Estimation for the AB-Model

The AB-model is completely defined by the following equations and distributional assumptions

$A\,\varepsilon_t = B e_t$ A and B invertible matrices of order n

$E(e_t) = [0]$ $E(e_t e'_t) = I$

$\varepsilon_t \sim I\,MN\,([0], \Sigma)$ $\det \Sigma \neq 0$

All the sample information is contained in the $\hat{\Sigma}$ matrix

$$\hat{\Sigma} = \frac{\hat{\varepsilon}\,\hat{\varepsilon}'}{T}$$

The corresponding log-likelihood function for the parameters of interest in the AB-model (the $2n^2$ parameters in the A and B matrices) is

$$\mathcal{L}(A,B) = c + T\log|A| - T\log|B| - \frac{T}{2}tr\left(A'B'^{-1}B^{-1}A\,\hat{\Sigma}\right) \tag{1}$$

We can write this log-likelihood also in the following form

$$\mathcal{L}(A,B) = c + T\log|K| - \frac{T}{2}tr(K'\,K\,\hat{\Sigma}) \tag{1b}$$

with $K = B^{-1}A$.

We assume that all the usual regularity conditions hold for this function, the associated density function and the "structural" parameter space.

Again the conditions

$A\,\Sigma\,A' = B\,B'$

naturally induce a set of non-linear restrictions on the parameter space (that now is a subset of R^{2n^2}) so, in general, necessary and sufficient condition can be obtained only for local identification.

In order to achieve identification, let us assume the parameters contained in matrices A and B are subject to two sets of separate constraints (in the following we will not examine the case of cross-restrictions on A and B parameters taken together).

$$R_a \, vecA = d_a \tag{2a}$$

$$R_b \, vecB = d_b \tag{2b}$$

or, in more compact form

$$\begin{bmatrix} R_a & [0] \\ [0] & R_b \end{bmatrix} \begin{bmatrix} vecA \\ vecB \end{bmatrix} = \begin{bmatrix} d_a \\ d_b \end{bmatrix} \tag{2}$$

where R_a is a $r_a \times n^2$ full row rank matrix and R_b is a $r_b \times n^2$ full row rank matrix while d_a is a $r_a \times 1$ possibly non zero vector and d_b is a $r_b \times 1$ possibly non zero vector.

In explicit form we have

$$vecA = S_a \gamma_a + s_a \tag{3a}$$

$$vecB = S_b \gamma_b + s_b \tag{3b}$$

or in more compact form

$$\begin{bmatrix} vecA \\ vecB \end{bmatrix} = \begin{bmatrix} S_a & [0] \\ [0] & S_b \end{bmatrix} \begin{bmatrix} \gamma_a \\ \gamma_b \end{bmatrix} + \begin{bmatrix} s_a \\ s_b \end{bmatrix} \tag{3}$$

where S_a is a $n^2 \times l_a$ full colomn rank matrix with $l_a = n^2 - r_a$ and s_a is a $n^2 \times 1$ vector, S_b is a $n^2 \times l_b$ full colomn rank matrix with $l_b = n^2 - r_b$ and s_b is a $n^2 \times 1$ vector and

$$R_a S_a = \underset{r_a \times l_a}{[0]} \qquad R_a s_a = d_a$$

$$R_b S_b = \underset{r_b \times l_b}{[0]} \qquad R_b s_b = d_b.$$

In order to geometrically analyze the local non identification situation in the absence of the a-priori information contained in system (2), we will compute the information matrix of the vectorized elements of the A and B matrices following this pattern of vectorization:

$$vec[A \mid B] = \begin{bmatrix} vecA \\ vecB \end{bmatrix}$$

without taking into account the set of linear restrictions (2) or (3).

Taking the following expression, we have

$$K = B^{-1} A$$

and calculating the differential

$$dK = (dB^{-1})\, A + B^{-1}\, dA$$

taking into account that (see Magnus and Neudecker 1988) the differential of dB^{-1} is equal to

$$dB^{-1} = -\,(B^{-1}\, dB\, B^{-1})$$

we have

$$dK = -\,(B^{-1}\, dB\, B^{-1})\, A + B^{-1}\, dA$$

which can be written in the following form

$$dK = B^{-1}\, dA + \left[-\,(B^{-1}\, dB\, B^{-1}\, A) \right]$$

Using the vec operator we get

$$dvecK = (I \otimes B^{-1})\, dvecA - (A'\, B'^{-1} \otimes B^{-1})\, dvecB$$

or, in partitioned matrix form

$$dvecK = \left[(I \otimes B^{-1}) \;\middle|\; -(A'\, B'^{-1} \otimes B^{-1}) \right] \begin{bmatrix} dvecA \\ dvecB \end{bmatrix}$$

This expression can be used to write the correctly defined matrix of partial derivatives (following appendix A usual notation rules)

$$\frac{\partial\, vecK}{\partial \begin{bmatrix} vecA \\ vecB \end{bmatrix}} = \left[(I \otimes B^{-1}) \;\middle|\; -(A'\, B'^{-1} \otimes B^{-1}) \right] \tag{4}$$

where (see Magnus and Neudecker 1988, p. 176),

$$\frac{\partial\, vecK}{\partial \begin{bmatrix} vecA \\ \hline vecB \end{bmatrix}} = \left[\frac{\partial\, vecK}{\partial\, vecA} \;\middle|\; \frac{\partial\, vecK}{\partial\, vecB} \right]$$

we can state that

$$\frac{\partial\, vecK}{\partial\, vecA} = (I \otimes B^{-1}) \tag{5}$$

$$\frac{\partial\, vecK}{\partial\, vecB} = -\,(A'B'^{-1} \otimes B^{-1}). \tag{6}$$

Remembering the chain rule of differentiation we can write

$$\frac{\partial\, \mathcal{L}(A,B)}{\partial \begin{bmatrix} vecA \\ \hline vecB \end{bmatrix}} = \frac{\partial\, \mathcal{L}}{\partial\, vecK} \frac{\partial\, vecK}{\partial \begin{bmatrix} vecA \\ \hline vecB \end{bmatrix}} = f' \begin{bmatrix} vecA \\ \hline vecB \end{bmatrix}$$

So the "score" vector of the log-likelihood function can be obtained in the following way

$$f' \begin{bmatrix} vecA \\ \hline vecB \end{bmatrix} = f'\,(vecK) \cdot \frac{\partial\, vecK}{\partial \begin{bmatrix} vecA \\ \hline vecB \end{bmatrix}}$$

$$f' \begin{bmatrix} vecA \\ \hline vecB \end{bmatrix} = f'\,(vecK) \cdot \left[(I \otimes B^{-1}) \;\middle|\; -\,(A'\,B'^{-1} \otimes B^{-1}) \right]$$

in row form, or

$$f \begin{bmatrix} vecA \\ \hline vecB \end{bmatrix} = \begin{bmatrix} I \otimes B'^{-1} \\ \hline -\,(B^{-1}\,A \otimes B'^{-1}) \end{bmatrix} f(vecK)$$

in column form.

The information matrix calculated with respect to the $(2n^2 \times 1)$ vector $\begin{bmatrix} vecA \\ \hline vecB \end{bmatrix}$

$$I_T \begin{bmatrix} vecA \\ \hline vecB \end{bmatrix} = E\left\{ f \begin{bmatrix} vecA \\ \hline vecB \end{bmatrix} \cdot f' \begin{bmatrix} vecA \\ \hline vecB \end{bmatrix} \right\},$$

can be calculated on the basis of $I_T\,(vecK)$ using the following expression:

$$I_T\left[\frac{vecA}{vecB}\right]=\left[\frac{I\otimes B'^{-1}}{-(B^{-1}A\otimes B'^{-1})}\right]I_T(vecK)\left[(I\otimes B^{-1})\;\middle|\;-(A'B'^{-1}\otimes B^{-1})\right]$$

From $\quad K=B^{-1}A$

we can write $\quad K'=A'B'^{-1}$

$$K^{-1}=A^{-1}B$$

$$K'^{-1}=B'A'^{-1}$$

and remembering that

$$I_T\,(vec\,K)=-T\cdot\left[K^{-1}\otimes I\right](I_{n^2}+\textcircled{T})\left[K'^{-1}\otimes I\right]$$

after some substitutions we can arrive at

$$I_T\left[\frac{vecA}{vecB}\right]=T\left[\frac{K^{-1}\otimes B'^{-1}}{-(I\otimes B'^{-1})}\right](I_{n^2}+\textcircled{T})\left[(K'^{-1}\otimes B^{-1})\;\middle|\;-(I\otimes B^{-1})\right]$$

The asymptotic information matrix, as usual, is

$$I\left[\frac{vecA}{vecB}\right]=\underset{T\to\infty}{plim}\frac{1}{T}I_T\left[\frac{vecA}{vecB}\right]$$

the matrix $\frac{1}{2}I\left[\frac{vecA}{vecB}\right]$ can be written in the following equivalent form

$$\frac{1}{2}I\left[\frac{vecA}{vecB}\right]=\left[\frac{K^{-1}\otimes B'^{-1}}{[0]}\;\middle|\;\frac{[0]}{-(I\otimes B'^{-1})}\right]\left[\frac{N_n}{N_n}\;\middle|\;\frac{N_n}{N_n}\right]\left[\frac{K'^{-1}\otimes B^{-1}}{[0]}\;\middle|\;\frac{[0]}{-(I\otimes B^{-1})}\right]$$

This matrix has the same rank as the matrix

$$\left[\frac{N_n}{N_n}\;\middle|\;\frac{N_n}{N_n}\right]$$

obviously equal to the rank of N_n and so equal to $n(n+1)/2$.

Taking into account the system of linear restrictions (2):

$$\left[\frac{R_a}{[0]}\;\middle|\;\frac{[0]}{R_b}\right]\left[\frac{vecA}{vecB}\right]=\left[\frac{d_a}{d_b}\right]$$

its derivative is simply

$$\left[\begin{array}{c|c} R_a & [0] \\ \hline [0] & R_b \end{array}\right]$$

On this basis we can construct the "augmented" information matrix (following Rothenberg 1971)

$$V\left[\frac{vecA}{vecB}\right]=\left[\begin{array}{c} I\left[\frac{vecA}{vecB}\right] \\ \hline \begin{array}{c|c} R_a & [0] \\ \hline [0] & R_b \end{array} \end{array}\right]$$

where

$$I\left[\frac{vecA}{vecB}\right]=2\left[\begin{array}{c|c} \dfrac{K^{-1}\otimes B'^{-1}}{[0]} & \dfrac{[0]}{-(I\otimes B'^{-1})} \end{array}\right]\left[\begin{array}{c|c} N_n & N_n \\ \hline N_n & N_n \end{array}\right]\left[\begin{array}{c|c} \dfrac{K'^{-1}\otimes B^{-1}}{[0]} & \dfrac{[0]}{-(I\otimes B^{-1})} \end{array}\right]$$

Using the usual trick we can premultiply by the block-diagonal invertible matrix

$$\frac{1}{2}\left[\begin{array}{c|c|c|c} K\otimes B' & [0] & [0] & [0] \\ \hline [0] & -[I\otimes B'] & [0] & [0] \\ \hline [0] & [0] & 2\,I_{r_a} & [0] \\ \hline [0] & [0] & [0] & 2\,I_{r_b} \end{array}\right]$$

and postmultiply by the block-diagonal invertible matrix

$$\left[\begin{array}{c|c} K'\otimes B & [0] \\ \hline [0] & -(I\otimes B) \end{array}\right],$$

arriving at the equivalent (ie, same rank) matrix

$$V^*\left[\frac{vecA}{vecB}\right]=\left[\begin{array}{c|c} N_n & N_n \\ \hline N_n & N_n \\ \hline R_a(K'\otimes B) & [0] \\ \hline [0] & R_b(I\otimes B) \end{array}\right].$$

From the property of the N_n matrix (see Magnus (1988) p. 49, property IV)

$$N_n\,(A\otimes A)=N_n(A\otimes A)N_n=(A\otimes A)N_n$$

if we postmultiply $V^*\left[\frac{vecA}{vecB}\right]$ by the following matrix

$$\left[\begin{array}{cc} (B'\otimes B') & [0] \\ [0] & (B'\otimes B') \end{array}\right]$$

by virtue of the fact that

$$\left[\frac{N_n}{N_n}\middle|\frac{N_n}{N_n}\right]\begin{bmatrix}(B'\otimes B') & [0]\\ [0] & (B'\otimes B')\end{bmatrix}=\begin{bmatrix}(B'\otimes B') & [0]\\ [0] & (B'\otimes B')\end{bmatrix}\left[\frac{N_n}{N_n}\middle|\frac{N_n}{N_n}\right],$$

premultiplying by the block-diagonal invertible matrix

$$\left[\begin{array}{c|c|c|c} B'^{-1}\otimes B'^{-1} & [0] & [0] & [0]\\ \hline [0] & B'^{-1}\otimes B'^{-1} & [0] & [0]\\ \hline [0] & [0] & I_{r_a} & [0]\\ \hline [0] & [0] & [0] & I_{r_b}\end{array}\right]$$

we arrive at the following equivalent matrix:

$$V^{**}\left[\frac{vecA}{vecB}\right]=\left[\begin{array}{c|c} \frac{N_n}{N_n} & \frac{N_n}{N_n}\\ \hline R_a(A'\otimes BB') & [0]\\ \hline [0] & R_b(B'\otimes BB')\end{array}\right].$$

The V, V^* and V^{**} matrices are obviously of the same order $(2n^2+r_a+r_b)\times 2n^2$ and have the same rank.

In order to obtain a necessary and sufficient condition for identification we must look for the rank of this matrix (the necessary and sufficient condition for identification is, as usual, that this matrix evaluated at the "true" value $\left[\frac{vecA_0}{vecB_0}\right]$ has full column rank $2n^2$).

Following arguments similar to the ones used for the K and C models, we will look at the system

$$\left[\begin{array}{c|c} \frac{N_n}{N_n} & \frac{N_n}{N_n}\\ \hline R_a(A'\otimes BB') & [0]\\ \hline [0] & R_b(B'\otimes BB')\end{array}\right]y=[0]$$

$$V^{**}\left[\frac{vecA}{vecB}\right]y=[0]$$

where y is a $2n^2\times 1$ column vector.

In order to find the necessary and sufficient conditions for having $y=[0]$ as the unique solution of the system, we can split the system into two connected systems

$$\left[\begin{array}{c|c} N_n & N_n \\ \hline N_n & N_n \end{array}\right] y = [0] \tag{7}$$

$$\left[\begin{array}{c|c} R_a(A'\otimes BB') & [0] \\ \hline [0] & R_b(B'\otimes BB') \end{array}\right] y = [0]. \tag{8}$$

Now, let us suppose that the y vector can be written as

$$\underset{2n^2\times 1}{y} = \left[\begin{array}{c} z \\ \hline v \end{array}\right]$$

where z and v are $n^2\times 1$ column vectors.

The two connected systems of equations (7) and (8) can be written as

$$\begin{cases} N_n z + N_n v = [0] \\ N_n z + N_n v = [0] \end{cases} \tag{7}$$

$$\begin{cases} R_a\,(A'\otimes BB')\,z = [0] \\ R_b\,(B'\otimes BB')\,v = [0] \end{cases} \tag{8}$$

looking at (7) we can see that

$$N_n\,(z+v) = [0]$$

is the only non-repeated matrix equation.

The general solution of this equation is

$$z + v = \underset{n^2\times n(n-1)/2}{\tilde{D}_n}\; x$$

$$z + v = vecW = \tilde{D}_n\, x,$$

where $W = -W'$ is an arbitrary skew-symmetric matrix.

By substituting in (8) we arrive at the two connected systems of equations

$$\begin{cases} R_a\,(A'\otimes BB')\,z = [0] \\ R_b\,(B'\otimes BB')\,(\tilde{D}_n\, x - z) = [0] \end{cases} \tag{9}$$

System (9) is a homogeneous system of $r_a + r_b$ equations in $n^2 + {}^{n(n-1)}\!/_2$ unknowns (n^2 unknowns for z and ${}^{n\,(n-1)}\!/_2$ for x respectively). A necessary condition for local identification is obviously that $r_a + r_b \geq n^2 + n(n-1)/2$. A necessary and sufficient condition can be stated in the following way:

Condition for identification in the AB-model

Assuming the invertibility of the A and B matrices, the "true" vector

$$\begin{bmatrix} vecA_0 \\ \hline vecB_0 \end{bmatrix}$$

is locally identified if and only if the system

$$\begin{cases} R_a\,(A'\otimes BB')\,z = [0] \\ R_b\,(B'\otimes BB')\,(\tilde{D}_n\,x - z) = [0] \end{cases}$$

evaluated at A_0 and B_0 has for x and z the unique solution:

$$x = [0]$$

$$z = [0]$$

Looking for conditions that can be easily numerically checked, we can take the first matrix equation in the preceding condition

$$R_a\,(A'\otimes BB')\,z = [0]$$

and look for its general solution which is simply

$$z = \left(A^{-1}\otimes (BB')^{-1}\right) S_a \cdot t$$

for every t.

We can now insert it in the second equation

$$R_b\,(B'\otimes BB')\,\tilde{D}_n\,x - \left[A^{-1}\otimes (BB')^{-1}\right] S_a \cdot t = [0]$$

and for B and A satisfying

$$vecA = S_a\,\gamma_a + s_a$$

$$vecB = S_b\,\gamma_b + s_b$$

we can check whether the system

$$R_b\,(B'\otimes BB')\left\{\tilde{D}_n \;\middle|\; -\left[A^{-1}\otimes(BB')^{-1}\right]S_a\right\}\left[\frac{x}{t}\right]=[0]$$

i.e., $Q\left[\frac{x}{t}\right]=[0]$

with $Q=R_b\,(B'\otimes BB')\left\{\tilde{D}_n \mid \left[A^{-1}\otimes(BB')^{-1}\right]S_a\right\}$

has the unique solution $\left[\frac{x}{t}\right]=[0]$ or equivalently whether the Q matrix properly constructed with "casual" values for γ_a and γ_b is of full column rank.

In appendix C, using the condition stated above, we will propose a symbolic analysis of some interesting cases.

Now, having found the condition for local identification, we can move on to the problem of F.I.M.L. estimation of the parameters through the score algorithm, remembering the restrictions on A and B in explicit form

$$vecA=S_a\,\gamma_a+s_a$$

$$vecB=S_b\,\gamma_b+s_b$$

$$\begin{bmatrix} vecA \\ vecB \end{bmatrix}=\begin{bmatrix} S_a & [0] \\ [0] & S_b \end{bmatrix}\begin{bmatrix} \gamma_a \\ \gamma_b \end{bmatrix}+\begin{bmatrix} s_a \\ s_b \end{bmatrix};$$

using the chain rule of differentiation

$$f'\left[\frac{\gamma_a}{\gamma_b}\right]=f'\left[\frac{vecA}{vecB}\right]\left\{\frac{\partial}{\partial\left(\frac{\gamma_a}{\gamma_b}\right)}\left[\frac{vecA}{vecB}\right]\right\}=$$

$$f'\left[\frac{\gamma_a}{\gamma_b}\right]=f'\left[\frac{vecA}{vecB}\right]\begin{bmatrix} S_a & [0] \\ [0] & S_b \end{bmatrix}$$

or in column form:

$$f\left[\frac{\gamma_a}{\gamma_b}\right]=\begin{bmatrix} S'_a & [0] \\ [0] & S'_b \end{bmatrix}f\left[\frac{vecA}{vecB}\right]$$

taking into account that the information matrix $I_T\left(\frac{\gamma_a}{\gamma_b}\right)$ is

$$I_T\left[\frac{\gamma_a}{\gamma_b}\right]=E\left\{f\left[\frac{\gamma_a}{\gamma_b}\right]\cdot f'\left[\frac{\gamma_a}{\gamma_b}\right]\right\}$$

$$I_T\begin{bmatrix}\gamma a\\ \gamma b\end{bmatrix}=\begin{bmatrix}S'a & [0]\\ [0] & S'b\end{bmatrix} I_T\begin{bmatrix}vecA\\ vecB\end{bmatrix}\begin{bmatrix}Sa & [0]\\ [0] & Sb\end{bmatrix}$$

and that the asymptotic information matrix is

$$I\begin{bmatrix}\gamma a\\ \gamma b\end{bmatrix}=\begin{bmatrix}S'a & [0]\\ [0] & S'b\end{bmatrix} I\begin{bmatrix}vecA\\ vecB\end{bmatrix}\begin{bmatrix}Sa & [0]\\ [0] & Sb\end{bmatrix}$$

using the information matrix $I_T\begin{pmatrix}\gamma a\\ \gamma b\end{pmatrix}$ and the score vector $f\begin{pmatrix}\gamma a\\ \gamma b\end{pmatrix}$ we can implement the score algorithm in order to find F.I.M.L. estimates of $\begin{pmatrix}\gamma a\\ \gamma b\end{pmatrix}$, say $\begin{pmatrix}\tilde{\gamma} a\\ \tilde{\gamma} b\end{pmatrix}$, using the usual updating formula

$$\begin{bmatrix}\gamma a\\ \gamma b\end{bmatrix}_{n+1}=\begin{bmatrix}\gamma a\\ \gamma b\end{bmatrix}_n+\left(I_T\begin{bmatrix}\gamma a\\ \gamma b\end{bmatrix}_n\right)^{-1}\cdot f\begin{bmatrix}\gamma a\\ \gamma b\end{bmatrix}_n$$

at the end of the recursion we can immediately obtain the F.I.M.L. estimates of $\begin{bmatrix}vecA\\ vecB\end{bmatrix}$, say $\begin{pmatrix}vec\tilde{A}\\ vec\tilde{B}\end{pmatrix}$, using

$$\begin{bmatrix}vec\tilde{A}\\ vec\tilde{B}\end{bmatrix}=\begin{bmatrix}Sa & [0]\\ [0] & Sb\end{bmatrix}\begin{bmatrix}\tilde{\gamma} a\\ \tilde{\gamma} b\end{bmatrix}+\begin{bmatrix}sa\\ sb\end{bmatrix}$$

Inserting the $\tilde{\gamma}a$, $\tilde{\gamma}b$ values in the information matrix $I_T\begin{pmatrix}\gamma a\\ \gamma b\end{pmatrix}$, we can immediately arrive at the estimated asymptotic variance covariance matrix of vector $\begin{pmatrix}\tilde{\gamma} a\\ \tilde{\gamma} b\end{pmatrix}$

$$A\hat{v}ar\left\{\sqrt{T}\left[\begin{pmatrix}\tilde{\gamma} a\\ \tilde{\gamma} b\end{pmatrix}-\begin{pmatrix}\gamma a\\ \gamma b\end{pmatrix}\right]\right\}=I\begin{pmatrix}\tilde{\gamma} a\\ \tilde{\gamma} b\end{pmatrix}^{-1}$$

and from this matrix through the Cramer linear transformation theorem to

$$A\hat{v}ar\left\{\sqrt{T}\left[\begin{pmatrix}vec\tilde{A}\\ vec\tilde{B}\end{pmatrix}-\begin{pmatrix}vecA\\ vecB\end{pmatrix}\right]\right\}=\begin{bmatrix}Sa & [0]\\ [0] & Sb\end{bmatrix} I\begin{bmatrix}\tilde{\gamma} a\\ \tilde{\gamma} b\end{bmatrix}^{-1}\begin{bmatrix}S'a & [0]\\ [0] & S'b\end{bmatrix}$$

and $\begin{pmatrix}vec\tilde{A}\\ vec\tilde{B}\end{pmatrix}$ is asymptotically normally distributed as

$$\begin{bmatrix} vec\tilde{A} \\ vec\tilde{B} \end{bmatrix} \sim AN\left\{ \begin{bmatrix} vecA \\ vecB \end{bmatrix}, \frac{1}{T}\begin{bmatrix} S_a & [0] \\ [0] & S_b \end{bmatrix} I \begin{bmatrix} \tilde{\gamma}_a \\ \tilde{\gamma}_b \end{bmatrix}^{-1} \begin{bmatrix} S'_a & [0] \\ [0] & S'_b \end{bmatrix} \right\}$$

Having obtained the F.I.M.L. estimates of A and B, $\tilde{A}$ and $\tilde{B}$, we can calculate the F.I.M.L. estimate of Σ:

$$\tilde{\Sigma} = \tilde{A}^{-1} \tilde{B} \tilde{B}' \tilde{A}'^{-1}$$

and in the usual way calculate a test for the over-identifying restrictions

$$LR = 2\, \mathcal{L}(\hat{\Sigma}) - 2\, \mathcal{L}(\tilde{\Sigma}).$$

distributed under H_0 as a χ^2 with a number of degrees of freedom equal to the number of over-identifying restrictions.

5. Impulse Response Analysis and Forecast Error Variance Decomposition in SVAR Modeling

5.a Impulse Response Analysis

The technique of impulse response analysis, first introduced in VAR modeling by Sims (1980), is a descriptive device representing the reaction of each variable to a shock in each equation of the system. "In order to be able to see the distinct pattern of movement the system may display" (Sims 1980, p. 21), the shocks must obviously be orthogonal.

This condition is never fulfilled in concrete situations; the researcher must therefore operate so as to orthogonalize VAR residuals.

In the 'usual' impulse response analysis "there is no unique best way to do this" (Sims 1980, p. 21); if one chooses a solution not explicitly based on economic theory, such as 'Cholesky decomposition', an incredible number[1] of impulse response functions have to be analyzed.

In SVAR modeling, once that a "structure" is identified and estimated, we are left with only one natural structure for our variables, so we need to examine only n^2 impulse response functions (n impulse response functions for each independent shock).

---

1 If one has a VAR model for n variables, $n \times n!$ impulse response functions should be analyzed; ie, $n\times$ all the possible fully recursive structures; $n!$ is in fact the number of all the possible different Cholesky decompositions of the variance covariance matrix of VAR residuals for all the possible orderings of the variables.

Another problem with "usual" impulse response analysis is that impulse response functions can rarely be provided with properly constructed confidence intervals[2].

On the basis of recent works by Lütkepohl (1989, 1990) for the "usual" impulse response analysis, we can obtain the asymptotic distributions of such functions for SVAR models.

Before moving to our proposal we must stress that SVAR modeling has an original drawback, which derives from VAR modeling and which structuralization cannot overcome.

VAR modeling is not a parsimonious modeling, by which it is meant that VAR models are usually over-parametrized. When confidence intervals are calculated (with Monte Carlo, bootstrapping or asymptotic methods) taking into proper account VAR parameters uncertainty, very large (see Runkle 1987) confidence intervals around the calculated impulse responses should hardly be a surprise (in addition to Runkle's (1987) paper see also its comment by Sims - interesting as ever - in the same issue of the journal).

There are several possible ways to correct the intrinsic over-parametrization of VAR models (see for example Lütkepohl (1991), chapter 5) but we will not discuss this topic any further here.

Once we have obtained consistent estimates of the parameters in the K, C, A, B matrices for the corresponding models, usual asymptotic properties assure convergence in distribution of the following vectors:

$$\sqrt{T}(vec\tilde{K} - vecK) \xrightarrow{d} N\left[[0], \Sigma_k\right], \qquad \text{(K-model)}$$

a consistent estimate of Σ_k is given by

$$\tilde{\Sigma}_k = S_k I(\tilde{\gamma}_k)^{-1} S'_k;$$

$$\sqrt{T}(vec\tilde{C} - vecC) \xrightarrow{d} N\left[[0], \Sigma_c\right], \qquad \text{(C-model)}$$

a consistent estimate of Σ_c is given by

---

2 The RATS package offers the opportunity to calculate impulse response confidence bounds through Monte Carlo integration technique, but bootstrapping can be used for the same purpose.

$\tilde{\Sigma}_c = S_c\, I(\tilde{\gamma}_c)^{-1} S'_c;$

$$\sqrt{T}\left[\begin{pmatrix} vec\tilde{A} \\ vec\tilde{B} \end{pmatrix} - \begin{pmatrix} vecA \\ vecB \end{pmatrix}\right] \xrightarrow{d} N\left[[0], \Sigma_{ab}\right], \qquad \text{(AB-model)}$$

and a consistent estimate of Σ_{ab} is given by

$$\tilde{\Sigma}_{ab} = \begin{bmatrix} S_a & [0] \\ [0] & S_b \end{bmatrix} \left\{ I \begin{bmatrix} \tilde{\gamma}_a \\ \tilde{\gamma}_b \end{bmatrix} \right\}^{-1} \begin{bmatrix} S'_a & [0] \\ [0] & S'_b \end{bmatrix}.$$

In what follows we will use the following theorem (see Serfling 1980, p. 122)[3].

Theorem: Suppose β is a $(n{\times}1)$ vector of parameters and $\hat{\beta}$ is an estimator such that

$$\sqrt{T}(\hat{\beta} - \beta) \xrightarrow{d} N\,([0], \Sigma).$$

Let $g(\beta) = \left[g_1(\beta), g_2(\beta), \ldots, g_m(\beta)\right]'$ be a continuously differentiable function with values in the m-dimensional Euclidean space and $\dfrac{\partial g_i}{\partial \beta} = \left[\dfrac{\partial g_i}{\partial \beta_1}, \ldots, \dfrac{\partial g_i}{\partial \beta_n}\right]$ be non zero at β for $i = 1, \ldots, m$. Then

$$\sqrt{T}[g(\hat{\beta}) - g(\beta)] \xrightarrow{d} N\left[[0], \frac{\partial g}{\partial \beta}\Sigma\left(\frac{\partial g}{\partial \beta}\right)'\right]$$

(where $\dfrac{\partial g}{\partial \beta}$ is a $m{\times}n$ matrix and $\left(\dfrac{\partial g}{\partial \beta}\right)'$ is a $n{\times}m$ matrix).

On the basis of this theorem we can calculate the distribution of $vec\tilde{K}^*$ where $\tilde{K}^* = \tilde{B}^{-1}\tilde{A}$, and $K^* = B^{-1}A$.

Starting from the distribution of $\begin{bmatrix} vec\tilde{A} \\ vec\tilde{B} \end{bmatrix}$ and remembering that

$$\frac{\partial\, vecK}{\partial \begin{pmatrix} vecA \\ vecB \end{pmatrix}} = \left[I \otimes B^{-1} \,\middle|\, -(A'B'^{-1} \otimes B^{-1}) \right]$$

3 Our formulation is substantially identical to Lütkepohl's (1990), minor changes are due to our modified differential notation. For a more rigorous treatment of the problem faced here and in the following pages see Serfling (1980) p. 118-125 and in particular Theorem A (p. 122) and the corollary (p. 124).

we can immediately arrive at

$$\sqrt{T}(vec\tilde{K}^* - vecK^*) \xrightarrow{d} N\left[[0], \Sigma_{k^*}\right]$$

where $vecK^* = vec(B^{-1}A)$

$$\Sigma_{k^*} = \left[I \otimes B^{-1} \middle| -(A'B'^{-1} \otimes B^{-1}) \right] \Sigma_{ab} \left[\frac{I \otimes B'^{-1}}{-(B^{-1}A \otimes B'^{-1})} \right]$$

and

$$\tilde{\Sigma}_{k^*} = \left[I \otimes \tilde{B}^{-1} \middle| -(\tilde{A}'\tilde{B}'^{-1} \otimes \tilde{B}^{-1}) \right] \tilde{\Sigma}_{ab} \left[\frac{I \otimes \tilde{B}'^{-1}}{-(\tilde{B}^{-1}\tilde{A} \otimes \tilde{B}'^{-1})} \right].$$

In order to arrive at the distribution of the calculated impulse response functions we need the distributions of

$vec(\tilde{K}^{-1})$ for the K-model

$vec(\tilde{C})$ for the C-model

$vec(\tilde{K}^{*-1})$ for the AB-model

While for the C-model the appropriate distribution was directly obtained, for the K and AB models we need again the theorem previously introduced and, since the inverse transformation is a continuous function of the elements of a matrix at any point where the matrix is not singular, starting from

$$\frac{\partial\, vecK^{-1}}{\partial\, vecK} = -\left(K'^{-1} \otimes K^{-1}\right)$$

$$\left(\frac{\partial\, vecK^{-1}}{\partial\, vecK}\right)' = -\left(K^{-1} \otimes K'^{-1}\right),$$

for the K-model we obtain

$$\sqrt{T}(vec\tilde{K}^{-1} - vecK^{-1}) \xrightarrow{d} N\left[[0], \Sigma_{k^{-1}}\right]$$

where

$$\Sigma_{k^{-1}} = (K'^{-1} \otimes K^{-1})\, \Sigma_k\, (K^{-1} \otimes K'^{-1}).$$

$$\tilde{\Sigma}_k^{-1} = (\tilde{K}'^{-1} \otimes \tilde{K}^{-1})\, \tilde{\Sigma}_k\, (\tilde{K}^{-1} \otimes \tilde{K}'^{-1}).$$

For the AB-model we can write

$$\sqrt{T}(vec\tilde{K}^{*-1} - vecK^{*-1}) \xrightarrow{d} N\left[[0], \Sigma_k^{*-1}\right]$$

where

$$\Sigma_k^{*-1} = (K^{*\prime-1} \otimes K^{*-1})\, \Sigma_k^*\, (K^{*-1} \otimes K^{*\prime-1})$$

$$\tilde{\Sigma}_k^{*-1} = (\tilde{K}^{*\prime-1} \otimes \tilde{K}^{*-1})\, \tilde{\Sigma}_k^*\, (\tilde{K}^{*-1} \otimes \tilde{K}^{*\prime-1})$$

(where $K^* = B^{-1}A$, and $\tilde{K}^* = \tilde{B}^{-1}\tilde{A}$).

With these formulae we can partially use the result by Lütkepohl (1989, 1990) with respect to the following inverted structuralized models:

$$y_t = \left[A(L)^{-1}\, K^{-1}\right] e_t \qquad \text{for the K-model}$$

$$y_t = \left[A(L)^{-1}\, C\right] e_t \qquad \text{for the C-model}$$

$$y_t = \left[A(L)^{-1}\, K^{*-1}\right] e_t \qquad \text{for the AB-model, where } K^* = B^{-1}A.$$

In order to simplify notation let us refer to

$$y_t = P(L)\, e_t = \sum_{i=0}^{\infty} P_i\, e_{t-i},$$

where

$$P(L) = \left[A(L)^{-1}\, K^{-1}\right] \qquad \text{for the K-model}$$

$$P(L) = \left[A(L)^{-1}\, C\right] \qquad \text{for the C-model}$$

$$P(L) = \left[A(L)^{-1}\, K^{*-1}\right] \qquad \text{for the AB-model, where } K^* = B^{-1}A$$

and

$$P_0 = K^{-1} \qquad \text{for the K-model}$$

$$P_0 = C \qquad \text{for the C-model}$$

$$P_0 = K^{*-1} \qquad \text{for the AB-model;}$$

let us call the following matrix A (see Lütkepohl 1989)

$$A = \begin{bmatrix} A_1 \; A_2 \ldots & A_{p-1} \; A_p \\ I_n \; 0 \ldots & 0 \quad 0 \\ 0 \ldots \ldots & \ldots \; \ldots \\ \ldots \ldots \ldots & \ldots \; \ldots \\ 0 \; 0 \ldots & I_n \quad 0 \end{bmatrix} (np \times np)$$

and $J = \left[I_n \mid [0] \mid \ldots \mid [0] \right]$ the $n \times np$ "extraction matrix".

In view of this notation, starting from the A_i values, the coefficient matrices of the "Structured" Moving Average representation (P_i) can be calculated with the two equivalent formulae

$$P_i = J\, A^i\, J'\, P_0 \quad i = 1, 2, \ldots$$

or recursively

$$\left. \begin{array}{l} P_i = C_i \cdot P_0 \\ C_i = \sum_{j=1}^{i} C_{i-j}\, A_j \end{array} \right\} i = 1, \ldots \text{ and } C_0 = I_n$$

In order to arrive at the asymptotic distribution of the estimated P_i we use the following additional notation:

$$\underset{n^2 p \times 1}{\pi} = vec\Pi = vec\left[A_1, A_2, \ldots, A_p \right]$$

$$p_i = vecP_i \qquad p_i \text{ is } n^2 \times 1$$

$$\underline{p}_h = vec\left[P_0, P_1, \ldots, P_h \right] \qquad \underline{p}_h \text{ is} \left[(h+1) n^2 \times 1 \right]$$

and

$$\sqrt{T}(\hat{p}_0 - p_0) \xrightarrow{d} N\,([0], \Sigma(0))$$

where $\Sigma(0)$ is respectively equal to

$$\Sigma(0) = \Sigma_k^{-1} \qquad \text{for the K-model}$$

$$\Sigma(0) = \Sigma_c \qquad \text{for the C-model}$$

$$\Sigma(0) = \Sigma_k^{*-1} \qquad \text{for the AB-model.}$$

Remembering that $\hat{\pi}$ and $\hat{p}_0$ under the conditions of the two-step logic are asymptotically normally independently distributed, following proposition 2 in Lütkepohl (1989), we have

$$\sqrt{T}(\hat{p}_h - p_h) \xrightarrow{d} N([0], \Sigma(h)).$$

In the above expression quantities are defined as follows: $\Sigma(h)$ is a $(h+1)n^2 \times (h+1)n^2$ matrix with the ij-th $n^2 \times n^2$ block

$$\Sigma(h)_{ij} = G_i \Sigma_\pi G'_j + (I_n \otimes J A^i J') \Sigma(0) (I_n \otimes J A^j J')';$$

using the notation introduced in section 1, Σ_π is the variance-covariance matrix of the following asymptotic distribution:

$$\sqrt{T}(vec\hat{\Pi} - vec\Pi) \xrightarrow{d} N\left([0], Q^{-1} \otimes \Sigma\right),$$

where the G_i matrices are of $n^2 \times n^2 p$ order, and

$$G_0 = [0],$$

$$G_i = \sum_{k=0}^{i-1} \left\{ \left[P'_0 \cdot J (A')^{i-1-k} \right] \otimes J A^k J' \right\} \quad \text{for } i>0$$

The $\Sigma(h)_{ii}$ $(n^2 \times n^2)$ block is the variance covariance matrix of the $\hat{p}_i$ $(n^2 \times 1)$ vector of "structuralized" impulse responses, where $\hat{p}_i = vec\hat{P}_i$. See Lütkepohl (1989), Baillie (1987).

Obviously, the estimated $\tilde{\Sigma}(h)$ matrices can be found by inserting appropriate estimated values for the K, C and AB models; for all the models the estimated $\hat{A}_i$ matrices are the same and the $\tilde{\Sigma}$ matrix in the estimated $\tilde{\Sigma}_\pi$ expression is

$$\tilde{\Sigma} = (\tilde{K}' \tilde{K})^{-1} \qquad \text{for the K-model}$$

$$\tilde{\Sigma} = \tilde{C} \tilde{C}' \qquad \text{for the C-model}$$

$$\tilde{\Sigma} = \tilde{A}^{-1} \tilde{B} \tilde{B}' \tilde{A}'^{-1} \qquad \text{for the AB-model}$$

The estimated impulse responses are obviously obtained inserting the appropriate estimated matrices in one of the two equivalent formulae

$$\hat{P}_i = J\,\hat{A}^i J'\,\hat{P}_0 \qquad i = 0, 1, \ldots$$

or

$$\left.\begin{aligned} \hat{P}_i &= \hat{C}_i \cdot \hat{P}_0 \\ \hat{C}_i &= \sum_{j=1}^{i} \hat{C}_{i-j} A_j \end{aligned}\right\} i = 1, \ldots \text{ and } \hat{C}_0 = I_n$$

The knowledge of vector $\hat{p}_h$ of the estimated impulse responses

$$\hat{p}_h = vec\left[\hat{P}_0, \hat{P}_1, \ldots, \hat{P}_h\right]$$

and of its associated joint (estimated) variance covariance matrix allows us to calculate proper asymptotic confidence intervals and to perform a number of tests (see Lütkepohl, 1989, 1990) connected to linear combinations of the elements of the $\hat{p}_h$ vector.

5.b Variance Decomposition

by Antonio Lanzarotti

The Forecast Error Variance Decomposition (FEVD) technique, introduced by Sims in his famous 1980 paper, is a basic tool providing complementary information for a better understanding of the relations between the variables of a VAR model.

Whenever analyses of impulse response functions are performed in order to explain how variables react over time to innovations in other ones, FEVD allows us to compare the role played by different variables in causing such reactions; FEVD techniques have been used in a number of SVAR applications. See, for example, Bernanke (1986), Blanchard (1989), Blanchard and Quah (1989) and Shapiro and Watson (1988).

A recent paper by Lütkepohl (1990) contains some results on the estimation of FEVD coefficients and their asymptotic distribution. It gives some rather complicated formulae referred to the generic element $w_{kj,s}$ which represents the portion of s-step forecast error variance of variable k accounted for by innovations in variable j.

This paragraph presents the same information in more compact and tractable form using earlier results of the present monograph on the asymptotic distribution of impulse response function coefficients.

With this purpose in mind we will introduce the Hadamard operator $\odot$ as defined in Magnus and Neudecker (1988) p. 45.

If $A = (a_{ij})$ and $B = (b_{ij})$ are matrices of the same order, say $m \times n$, then $A \odot B$ gives a matrix of dimension $m \times n$ whose ij-th element equals $a_{ij} \cdot b_{ij}$.

The following properties can be easily derived from this definition:

a) $A \odot B = B \odot A$

b) $A \odot I_m = dgA$ if A has dimension $m \times m$

c) $vec(A \odot B) = vecA \odot vecB$

d) $$vecA \odot vecB = [(vecA\ u') \odot I_{mn}]vecB = D(A) \cdot vecB$$
$$= [(vecB\ u') \odot I_{mn}]vecA = D(B) \cdot vecA$$

where dgA is a matrix with diagonal equal to that of A and zero elsewhere;

u is a column vector of dimension $n \cdot m$ whose elements are all equal to one;

$D(A)$ is a matrix with diagonal elements equal to those of $vecA$ and zero elsewhere. This property is not contained in Magnus and Neudecker (1988). However it can be easily shown by noting that $[(vecA \cdot u') \odot I_{mn}]$ is a matrix whose diagonal elements are equal to those of $vecA$ and whose other elements are all equal to zero. Notice that this matrix - hereafter denoted by $D(A)$ - radically differs from dgA.

The first step of our procedure calculates a matrix of dimension $n \times n$ - denoted by W_s - whose elements are $w_{kj,s}$, with $k = 1, \ldots, n$.

Here follows the definition of $w_{kj,s}$ as proposed by Lütkepohl (1990):

$$w_{kj,s} = \sum_{i=0}^{s-1} \frac{p_{kj,i}^2}{MSE_k(s)}$$

$$MSE_k(s) = \sum_{i=0}^{s-1} e'_k C_i \Sigma C'_i e_k$$

where $p_{kj,i}$ is the kj-th element of P_i and e_k is the k-th column of I.

The matrix whose kj-th element is $\sum_{i=0}^{s-1} p_{kj,i}^2$ is as follows:

$$M_s = \sum_{i=0}^{s-1} P_i \odot P_i$$

By multiplying every row of M_s by the corresponding $\left[MSE_k(s)\right]^{-1}$ we obtain the FEVD coefficients. In other words, we must premultiply M_s by F_s^{-1}, where F_s is a diagonal matrix whose non-zero elements are $MSE_k(s)$. Remembering that

$$\Sigma = P_0 P'_0$$

we can write[4]:

$$MSE_k(s) = \sum_{i=0}^{s-1} e'_k C_i P_0 P'_0 C'_i e_k = \sum_{i=0}^{s-1} e'_k P_i P'_i e_k$$

Obviously, the matrix $\sum_{i=0}^{s-1} P_i P'_i$ has the corresponding $MSE_k(s)$ on its diagonal, hence:

$$F_s = dg\left(\sum_{i=0}^{s-1} P_i P'_i\right)$$

In view of property b) of the Hadamard product we can write:

$$F_s = \left(\sum_{i=0}^{s-1} P_i P'_i\right) \odot I_n$$

Now it follows that:

---

4 P_o is K^{-1} for the K-model, C for the C-model, $A^{-1}B$ for the AB-model

$$W_s = F_s^{-1} M_s \qquad \text{for } s = 1,\dots,h+1$$

h=order of the "calculated" VMA representation.

(Notice that the sum of the elements of each row of W_s is equal to one).

W_s is a matrix which depends only on the structured impulse response functions, whose asymptotic distribution is already known. We can therefore provide the distribution of $vecW_s$ using the theorem contained in Serfling (1980) (see also paragraph 5.a in this monograph). On the basis of this result, all we need to know is

$$Z_s = \frac{\partial\, vecW_s}{\partial\, \underline{p}_h} \qquad \text{where } \underline{p}_h = vec\,[P_0 \mid P_1 \mid \dots \mid P_h]$$

Thus if

$$\sqrt{T}\,(\hat{\underline{p}}_h - \underline{p}_h) \xrightarrow{d} N\,([0], \Sigma(h))$$

where the form of matrix $\Sigma(h)$ is defined block by block in the present section, then it follows that

$$\sqrt{T}\,(vec\hat{W}_s - vecW_s) \xrightarrow{d} N\left([0], Z_s\Sigma(h)Z_s'\right)$$

In order to compute Z_s it must be noticed that

$$Z_s = \frac{\partial\, vecW_s}{\partial\, \underline{p}_h} = \frac{\partial\, vecW_s}{\partial\, vec\,[P_0 \mid P_1 \mid \dots \mid P_h]} =$$

$$= \left[\frac{\partial\, vecW_s}{\partial\, vecP_0} \;\middle|\; \frac{\partial\, vecW_s}{\partial\, vecP_1} \;\middle|\; \cdots \;\middle|\; \frac{\partial\, vecW_s}{\partial\, vecP_h} \right]$$

On the basis of this last result we may proceed with the calculation of

$$\frac{\partial\, vecW_s}{\partial\, vecP_j} \qquad s = 1, \dots, h+1;\ j = 0, \dots, h$$

Obviously, whenever $j \geq s$, W_s does not depend on P_j. In such cases the following applies:

$$\frac{\partial\, vecW_s}{\partial\, vecP_j} = \underset{(n^2 x n^2)}{[0]}$$

Whenever this derivative is not equal to [0], we will use a "computational strategy" based on the following chain rule of differentiation (see Magnus and Neudecker (1988), chapter 8):

$$\frac{\partial\, vecW_s}{\partial\, vecP_j}=\frac{\partial\, vecW_s}{\partial\, vec(M_s \mid F_s)}\cdot\frac{\partial\, vec(M_s \mid F_s)}{\partial\, vecP_j}$$

Let us begin with the first factor of this product. Remembering that

$$W_s = F_s^{-1} M_s$$

differentiating, we obtain

$$d\,W_s = (dF_s^{-1})\, M_s + F_s^{-1}\,(dM_s)$$

$$d\,W_s = -F_s^{-1}\,(dF_s)\, F_s^{-1} M_s + F_s^{-1}\,(dM_s)$$

the vec notation is

$$dvecW_s = -\left(M'_s F_s'^{-1} \otimes F_s^{-1}\right) dvecF_s + (I \otimes F_s^{-1})\; dvecM_s$$

$$dvecW_s = \left[(I \otimes F_s^{-1}) \mid -(W_s' \otimes F_s^{-1})\right] dvec\,(M_s \mid F_s)$$

$$\frac{\partial\, vecW_s}{\partial\, vec(M_s \mid F_s)} = \left[(I \otimes F_s^{-1}) \mid -(W_s' \otimes F_s^{-1})\right]$$

Now $\dfrac{\partial\, vec(M_s \mid F_s)}{\partial\, vecP_j}$ must be calculated.

This matrix can be represented as being composed of two $n^2 \times n^2$ blocks and organized as follows

$$\begin{bmatrix} \dfrac{\partial\, vecM_s}{\partial\, vecP_j} \\ \dfrac{\partial\, vecF_s}{\partial\, vecP_j} \end{bmatrix}$$

It is easy to note that

$$\frac{\partial\, vecM_s}{\partial\, vecP_j} = \frac{\partial}{\partial\, vecP_j}\, vec \sum_{i=0}^{s-1} (P_i \odot P_i) = \frac{\partial}{\partial\, vecP_j}\, vec(P_j \odot P_j)$$

Let us calculate this last derivative starting from the differential

$$d\,(P_j \odot P_j) = (dP_j) \odot P_j + P_j \odot (dP_j)$$

on the basis of property a) of the Hadamard product we can write

$$d\,(P_j \odot P_j) = 2\,P_j \odot (dP_j)$$

or, in vec form,

$$d\,vec(P_j \odot P_j) = 2\,vecP_j \odot (d\,vecP_j)$$

On the basis of property d) we can write

$$d\,vec(P_j \odot P_j) = 2\,D(P_j)\,(d\,vecP_j) = 2\left[(vecP_j \cdot u') \odot I_{n^2}\right](d\,vecP_j)$$

Therefore we can conclude that

$$\frac{\partial\,vec(M_s)}{\partial\,vecP_j} = 2\,D(P_j)$$

where $D(P_j)$ is the same matrix previously obtained with diagonal elements equal to those of $vecP_j$ and zero elsewhere.

The same applies to the second block

$$\frac{\partial\,vecF_s}{\partial\,vecP_j} = \frac{\partial}{\partial\,vecP_j}\,vec\sum_{i=0}^{s-1}(P_iP_i' \odot I) = \frac{\partial}{\partial\,vecP_j}\,vec(P_j\,P_j' \odot I)$$

By applying the usual chain rule of differentiation, we can now decompose this derivative into two factors as follows:

$$\frac{\partial}{\partial\,vecP_j}\,vec(P_j\,P_j' \odot I) = \frac{\partial}{\partial\,(vecP_jP_j')}\,vec(P_j\,P_j' \odot I) \cdot \frac{\partial\,(vecP_jP_j')}{\partial vecP_j}$$

Imposing $Y = P_j\,P_j'$ we can calculate $\frac{\partial}{\partial\,vecY}\,vec\,(Y \odot I)$

$$d\,(Y \odot I) = (dY) \odot I$$

$$d\,vec(Y \odot I) = dvecY \odot vecI$$

$$d\,vec(Y \odot I) = D(I) \cdot dvecY$$

We therefore obtain

$$\frac{\partial}{\partial\,(vecP_i\,P_j{}')}\,vec\sum_{i=0}^{s-1}(P_iP_i{}'\odot I)=D(I).$$

Taking into consideration that

$$\frac{\partial\,(vecP_jP_j{}')}{\partial vecP_j}=(I_n{}^2+\textcircled{T})\,(P_j\otimes I)$$

we can conclude that

$$\frac{\partial\;vecF_s}{\partial\;vecP_j}=D(I)\,(I_n{}^2+\textcircled{T})\,(P_j\otimes I)=D(I)\;2N_n\,(P_j\otimes I),$$

where N_n, as in the previous chapters, is defined as

$$\frac{1}{2}\,(I_n{}^2+\textcircled{T}).$$

Now all the results obtained must be put together, thus recomposing the chain of derivatives we have just calculated

$$\frac{\partial\;vecW_s}{\partial\;vecP_j}=\left[(I\otimes F_s{}^{-1})\mid-(W'_s\otimes F_s{}^{-1})\right]\left[\frac{2\,D(P_j)}{D(I)\;2N_n\,P_j\otimes I)}\right]$$

or, in equivalent form,

$$\frac{\partial\;vecW_s}{\partial\;vecP_j}=2\left[(I\otimes F_s{}^{-1})D(P_j)-(W'_s\otimes F_s{}^{-1})D(I)(N_n)(P_j\otimes I)\right]$$

Let us not forget that, for the reasons already explained, this formula holds only if $j<s$ and that this derivative is otherwise equal to [0]. On the basis of this last result, we can now construct matrix Z_s which corresponds to

$$\frac{\partial\;vecW_s}{\partial\;\underline{p}_h}=\left[\;\frac{\partial\;vecW_s}{\partial\;vecP_0}\;\middle|\;\frac{\partial\;vecW_s}{\partial\;vecP_1}\;\middle|\;\cdots\;\middle|\;\frac{\partial\;vecW_s}{\partial\;vecP_h}\;\right]$$

The asymptotic variance-covariance matrix of $vecW_s$ can be obtained by the formula

$$\Sigma(W_s)=Z_s\,\Sigma(h)\,Z'_s$$

Obviously, the estimate of this matrix can be obtained by substituting the P_j matrices with their $\hat{P}_j$ estimates in all the formulae.

6. Long-run A-priori Information. Deterministic Components. Cointegration

6.a Long-run A-priori Information

In practical applications of Structural VAR Modeling, the most interesting theoretical constraints on the parameter space of matrices K, C, A and B probably come from some long-run considerations (see for example Blanchard and Quah (1989) for a very simple model of the C-class).

For the K-model, remembering that

$$A(L)\, y_t = \varepsilon_t$$

$$K\,\varepsilon_t = e_t$$

a class of typical long-run considerations could be inserted looking at the "structured" matrix of total multipliers of the observable (y_t) variables.

Calling

$$A(1) = I - A_1 - \ldots - A_p$$

the matrix of "unstructured" total multipliers of y_t variables and calling

$$A^*(1) = K\,A(1)$$

the matrix of "structured" total multipliers of the same variables, identification may be achieved by imposing particular constant values in some places of the structured $A^*(1)$ matrix. For example, for $n = 2$ we might consider

$$K\,A(1) = \begin{bmatrix} * & 0 \\ * & * \end{bmatrix} = A^*(1)$$

where the asterisks inside matrices denote non-constrained values.

Thus, in order to achieve identification we have introduced the theoretical consideration that the total multiplier of the first variable y_{1t} with respect to movements of the second variable y_{2t} must be zero.

This a-priori consideration algebraically implies that the inner product of the first row of the K matrix multiplied by the second column of the $A(1)$ matrix is zero.

In the general case for $n>2$ this constraint together with other constraints can always be represented with the usual formula

$$R\ vecK = d$$

remembering that a row (some rows in the case of a number of long-run constraints) of the R matrix contains elements of the $A(1)$ matrix and zero elsewhere.

But in our context this type of constraint typically introduces a number of cross (bilinear) restrictions between the parameters of the Π matrix (previously introduced) and the parameters of the K matrix.

In view of these cross (bilinear) restrictions the asymptotic information matrix

$$I\begin{bmatrix} vec\Pi \\ \hline vecK \end{bmatrix}$$

can no longer be assumed to be conveniently block diagonal, therefore the two-stage logic so frequently used until now for identification and estimation purposes loses its correct asymptotic statistical basis.

If we still try to use the two stage set-up we must remember that some elements of the R matrix must be taken as a random variable instead of as a constant. Thus, instead of

$$R\ vecK = d$$

in a two-stage set-up we must work with an inexact system of constraints

$$\hat{R}\ vecK = d$$

which will hold exactly in the limit, provided the estimated elements of the $\hat{R}$ matrix are consistent estimates of the "true" elements:

$$plim\,\hat{R} = R$$

The same obviously holds if we try to insert long-run constraints for the C-model, denoting[1]

$$C(1) = I + C_1 + C_2 + \ldots$$

the matrix of total multipliers of "unstructured" shocks ε_t and

$$C^*(1) = C(1)\,C$$

the matrix of "structured" multipliers of structured shocks e_t.

Great complications arise in our set-up if we consider unstructured VAR Modeling as the natural starting point for Structural VAR Analysis, thus retaining two-stage logic.

The difficulties connected with the treatment of this problem are clearly depicted in Pagan (1986), a paper devoted to the properties of two-stage estimators.

As Pagan suggests, the theory of quasi-maximum likelihood estimation (White 1982) seems to be a natural tool in order to correctly analyze the problem[2].

Looking at White's (1982) A1-A6 lists of assumptions on the basis of his Theorem 3.1, one can immediately see that for the K model, also in the presence of misspecification, the conditions for identification of Theorem 1 in Rothenberg (1971) are the same.

On the basis of Theorem 1 in Pagan (1986) assuming the strong consistency of our estimator of $vec\Pi$

$$vec\hat{\Pi} \xrightarrow{a.s.} vec\Pi$$

it can be shown that our estimator of $vecK$, locally identified for the K model, keeps its consistency under the type of misspecification presented here.

---

1 If the usual stationarity conditions $C(1) = A(1)^{-1}$ hold

2 White (1983) shows why our two stage set-up can be treated as his two stage quasi-maximum likelihood estimation logic (pp. 2.16, 2.17) and why two stage quasi-maximum likelihood estimation can be subsumed in the study of quasi-maximum likelihood estimation (pp. 3-11 and ff.).

In our framework, major complications arise in a quasi-maximum likelihood context for the identification and estimation of the C and AB-models.

All the results in our set-up draw heavily on the so-called Information matrix equivalence (see White (1982) p. 7)

$$I_T(\theta) = -E\left[\frac{\partial^2 \mathcal{L}}{\partial \theta \, \partial \theta'}\right] = E\left[\frac{\partial \mathcal{L}}{\partial \theta'} \cdot \frac{\partial \mathcal{L}}{\partial \theta}\right], \text{ with } \underset{k \times 1}{\theta}$$

In the presence of misspecification, however, such equivalence breaks down and can be asymptotically restated only in the case of asymptotic negligibility of misspecifications[3].

In view of these problems, we will proceed with the two-stage logic - even if the R matrix naturally contains some (strongly consistent) estimated elements - as if the $\hat{R}$ matrix were a "true" matrix instead of a matrix with some estimated parameters[4].

In doing so a warning must be introduced. Starting from the assumptions that the estimator of $vec\Pi$ is strongly consistent, and that long-run restrictions are "true", one can heuristically show that the estimates of the K, C, A and B matrices, previously introduced, are consistent. Nevertheless, the associated asymptotic variance covariance matrices[5] surely risk to be "poor" substitutes to correctly calculated asymptotic variance covariance matrices which would take into proper account the inexact nature of the

$$\hat{R}\, vecK = d$$

a-priori constraints for the K model, or similar constraints for the C and A-B models.

---

3 Other complications arise when trying to find correct formulae for the calculation of impulse response functions in order to take into account the presence of a non-null asymptotic covariance matrix between $vec\hat{\Pi}$ and $vec\hat{K}$

4 The natural inefficiency of the estimates $vec\hat{\Pi}$ of the first stage and a consequent incorrect use of the Cramer Rao lower bound must be taken into consideration.

5 The author is carrying out further research on this subject also in the direction outlined by Pagan's (1986) Theorem 7 in order to find a fully efficient estimator constructed in two-step and based on Rothenberg and Leenders (1964).

6.b Deterministic Components

Looking at the hypothesis introduced in chapter 1,

$$A(L)\, y_t = \varepsilon_t$$

$$y_t = C(L)\, \varepsilon_t$$

we have so far implicitly assumed that vector y_t has zero mean

$$E(y_t) = [0]$$

The assumption was made for convenience: the analysis developed so far would remain valid with only minor modifications if we assumed that the vector of stochastic variables behaves in a strictly stationary fashion around a vector of deterministic components

$$y_t = d_t + C(L)\, \varepsilon_t$$

where d_t may contain (for example) polynomial trends, seasonal dummies and dummies for outliers.

A common practice is to remove these components series by series, estimating their parameters by OLS methods and then estimating the VAR model.

In view of the results put forward by Nelson and Kang (1981) and taking into account that using these new tools in order to find theoretically sound interpretations of cyclical movements of macroeconomic aggregates is one of the main goals of Structural VAR Analysis, it is clear that we should not run the risk of introducing spurious periodicities.

In order to prevent spurious periodicity, the parameters of deterministic components should be estimated together with the autoregressive parameters in the VAR set-up.

Assuming that the $C(L)$ matrix of the Wold-like representation can be inverted giving as a result a finite p-order polynomial autoregressive matrix $A(L)$, from

$$y_t = d_t + C(L)\, \varepsilon_t$$

we can arrive at

$$A(L)\, y_t = A(L)\, d_t + \varepsilon_t$$

let

$$d_t^* = A(L)\, d_t$$

For example, in the case of a vector of deterministic linear trends:

$$d_t = \alpha + \beta t,$$

we would have

$$d_t^* = A(L)\, d_t = a + bt.$$

The vector autoregression with deterministic components can be written in extended explicit form as

$$y_t = A_1\, y_{t-1} + \ldots + A_p\, y_{t-p} + [\, a \mid b\,] \begin{bmatrix} 1 \\ \overline{t} \end{bmatrix} + \varepsilon_t$$

In compact form we can write

$$y_t = \Pi\, x_t + \varepsilon_t,$$

where $x_t = \left[y'_{t-1}, y'_{t-2}, \ldots, y'_{t-p} \mid 1, t \right]'$

and the Π matrix can be thought as composed of two distinct parts

$$\Pi = \left[\, \Pi_1 \middle| \Pi_2 \right],$$

where

$$\Pi_1 = \left[\, A_1 \middle| \, A_2 \middle| \ldots \middle| A_p \right]$$

$$\Pi_2 = [\, a \mid b]$$

and then proceed to the estimation in the usual way following section 1 notation:

$$\hat{\Pi} = YX'(XX')^{-1}$$

$$\hat{\Sigma} = \frac{\hat{V}\hat{V}'}{T}$$

where

$$\hat{V} = Y - \hat{\Pi} X$$

Denoting with D_T the matrix

$$\begin{bmatrix} \frac{1}{\sqrt{T}} I_{np} & [0] & [0] \\ [0] & \frac{1}{\sqrt{T}} & [0] \\ [0] & [0] & \frac{1}{\sqrt{T^3}} \end{bmatrix}$$

the following relation holds:

$$\text{plim } D_T X X' D_T = Q^*$$

where Q^* is a positive definite matrix.

Rescaled by the D_T matrix, the asymptotic distribution of the VAR parameters is given by:

$$\left(D_T^{-1} \otimes I\right)(vec\hat{\Pi} - vec\Pi) \xrightarrow{d} N\left([0], Q^{*-1} \otimes \Sigma\right)$$

noting that

$$\Pi_1 = \left[\, \Pi_1 \middle| \Pi_2 \right] \begin{bmatrix} I_{np} \\ [0] \end{bmatrix} = \Pi \begin{bmatrix} I_{np} \\ [0] \end{bmatrix}$$

and calling

$$\bar{J} = \begin{bmatrix} I_{np} \\ [0] \end{bmatrix}$$

using the properties of vec operator

$$vec\Pi_1 = vec(\Pi \bar{J}) = (\bar{J}' \otimes I) vec\Pi$$

from which

$$(\bar{J}' \otimes I)\left(D_T^{-1} \otimes I\right)\left(vec\hat{\Pi}_1 - vec\Pi_1\right) \xrightarrow{d} N\left([0], (\bar{J}' \otimes I)\left(Q^{*-1} \otimes \Sigma\right)(\bar{J} \otimes I)\right)$$

or more compactly

$$(\bar{J}' \otimes I)\left(D_T^{-1} \otimes I\right)\left(vec\hat{\Pi}_1 - vec\Pi_1\right) \xrightarrow{d} N\left([0], \left(\bar{J}'\, Q^{*-1}\, \bar{J} \otimes \Sigma\right)\right)$$

Noting that:

$$(\bar{J}' \otimes I)\left(D_T^{-1} \otimes I\right) = \sqrt{T}\, I_{np}$$

we can get the following asymptotic distribution

$$\sqrt{T}\left(vec\hat{\Pi}_1 - vec\Pi_1\right)\xrightarrow{d} N\left([0], \left(\bar{J}' Q^{*-1}\bar{J}\otimes\Sigma\right)\right)$$

whose variance-covariance matrix is consistently estimated by:

$$T\cdot\bar{J}'(XX')^{-1}\bar{J}'\otimes\hat{\Sigma}$$

Looking at the results of section 5, we must insert our Π_1 matrix with its associated asymptotic variance covariance matrix instead of the Π matrix in those formulae.

Obviously, the impulse response functions must be seen as impulse responses around a deterministic trend. For each series the deterministic trend around which the impulse response functions fluctuate ($\alpha_i + \beta_i\cdot t$, $i = 1\ldots n$) can obviously be estimated by OLS methods, one series at a time, in a consistent way if the series are truly stationary around a trend.

Similar reasoning and formulae must be used in the presence of other types of deterministic components such as seasonal dummies, dummies for outliers and intercept regime changes, obviously with a connected reasoning in the interpretation of impulse response functions.

6.c Cointegration

Fortunately, Structural VAR Analysis is not to be confined in the realm of stationarity (or first order non-stationarity, partially treated under paragraph b in this section). In fact it can be extended to non-stationary contexts where a consistent estimate of VAR parameters can be obtained; see Sims-Stock-Watson (1990) for vector autoregressions with a "rich" deterministic part and unit roots in the $A(L)$ matrix and Tsay and Tiao (1986) for roots on the unit circle for the $A(L)$ matrix.

The analysis of the K, C and AB models is exactly the same as the one exposed before, up to the end of section 4.

The difficulties arise when we try to analyze the distributional characteristics of impulse response functions in view of the fact that, in the presence of unit roots, VAR parameters, though consistently estimated, are typically non-standard distributed.

Under the hypothesis of cointegration (Engle-Granger 1987) the situation is made simpler (see also Johansen (1988, 1989a, 1989b) and for a review Hylleberg-Mizon (1989)).

Let us assume we have a vector of processes

$$y_t$$

where each element y_{it} is a so-called $I(1)$ process[6] and also that

$$(1-L)\, y_t = \Delta y_t$$

is a vector of jointly strictly stationary processes without any deterministic part possessing a Wold representation

$$\Delta y_t = C(L)\, \varepsilon_t$$

where ε_t is a multivariate normally distributed vector white noise with

$$E(\varepsilon_t\, \varepsilon'_t) = \Sigma,\ det(\Sigma) \neq 0.$$

Furthermore let us assume that the vector of $I(1)$ variables y_t has a finite (p-order) autoregressive representation

$$A(L)\, y_t = \varepsilon_t$$

Under the hypothesis of cointegration the $A(1)$ matrix

$$A(1) = I - A_1 - A_2 - \ldots - A_p$$

is singular and can be written as the product of two rectangular matrices

$$\underset{n\times n}{A(1)} = \underset{n\times r}{\gamma}\, \underset{r\times n}{\alpha'}$$

where γ and α are full column rank matrices and r is the so-called cointegrating rank (ie, the number of independent cointegrating vectors) and $\alpha' y_t$ is a $r\times 1$ vector of $I(0)$ variables.

In a recent paper Lütkepohl and Reimers (1990), taking into explicit account the cointegrating restrictions on the $A(1)$ matrix (following Johansen's F.I.M.L. approach), calculated the asymptotic distribution of

---

6 Following Engle and Granger (1987), we call $I(1)$ a process whose difference Δy_{it} has a stationary and invertible ARMA representation.

$$\left[\tilde{A}_1 \dots \tilde{A}_p\right] = \tilde{\Pi}$$

(where $\tilde{\Pi}$ stands for Johansen F.I.M.L. estimation), demonstrating the asymptotic normality of $\sqrt{T}(vec\tilde{\Pi} - vec\Pi)$ (see Lütkepohl and Reimers, 1990, pp. 7-8).

If the cointegrating restrictions on the $A(1)$ matrix are not explicitly imposed, the usual A.L.S. (Asymptotic Least Squares) formulae can still be used for the estimation of Π

$$\hat{\Pi} = YX'(XX')^{-1}$$

giving a consistent estimate of the $A_1 \dots A_p$ coefficient matrices and, on the basis of the results in Park and Phillips (1987) and Sims, Stock and Watson (1990), we can assume that $\sqrt{T}(vec\hat{\Pi} - vec\Pi)$ asymptotically possesses a zero mean normal distribution with a singular covariance matrix (Park and Phillips, 1987, p. 37) that, from a sampling point of view, can be approximated by the usual formula (see Park and Phillips, 1987, proposition 5.4)

$$(XX')^{-1} \otimes \hat{\Sigma}.$$

On the basis of these results Lütkepohl and Reimers have demonstrated that the coefficients of the $\hat{A}(L)^{-1}$ matrix (calculated with the usual formulae)

$$\hat{\Phi}_h = \sum_{m=1}^{h} \hat{\Phi}_{h-m} \hat{A}_m \qquad h = 1, 2, \dots$$

$$\Phi_0 = I$$

also have asymptotic normal distributions, and so the setting for "structural" impulse response analysis proposed in chapter 5 of this monograph still holds.

Obviously some differences do exist with respect to the stationary case.

The coefficients of Φ_h matrices and those of P_h "structuralized" (see chapter 5) impulse response matrices "will in general not die out in the long run. In other words [they] may be permanent rather than transitory. Therefore the Φ_h and P_h cannot be interpreted as unstructured or "structured" MA coefficient matrices and their sum will in general not be finite" (Lütkepohl and Reimers (1990), p. 3).

Lütkepohl and Reimers suggest that in a cointegrated context it may be advantageous to impose rank constraints on the $A(1)$ matrix in order to isolate equilibrium relationships. On the basis of the results of Phillips (1991), a stronger stance can be hold on this point. Phillips has shown that, in a cointegrating context, unrestricted VAR estimation leads to asymptotically biased estimates of any base of the cointegration space. Then, if one must pursue optimal inference in a cointegrated system, a F.I.M.L. set-up must be used and, starting from Lütkepohl and Reimers (1990) formulae, following the same reasoning contained in section 5, the distribution needed for dynamic simulation analysis (corresponding to this optimal strategy) could be easily calculated.

In order to leave unchanged the procedures of Appendix D also in the case of cointegrated variables, the following sub-optimal but not completely inefficient strategy could be suggested.

In our two stage set-up we could use, for example, Johansen F.I.M.L. technique in order to find rank constraints on the $A(1)$ matrix:

$$A(1) = \gamma\,\alpha'$$

where γ and α are $n{\times}r$ full column rank matrices.

Still in the first stage we must solve an identification problem connected to the isolation of r theoretically meaningful independent cointegrating vectors corresponding to r long-run relationships.

Note that:

$$A(1) = \gamma\, Q^{-1}\, Q\, \alpha' = \gamma_0\, \alpha_0'$$

$$\gamma_0 = \gamma\, Q^{-1}$$

$$\alpha_0' = Q\, \alpha'$$

where Q is an arbitrary, invertible $r{\times}r$ matrix.

If we reasonably charge the identification effort on the α' matrix, in the α_0' (structured) matrix only $(n{\times}r) - r^2$ free elements should appear.

For simplicity, let us concentrate on the exact identification of r theoretically meaningful long-run relationships, whose parameters could be thought as laying in the rows of the α_0'

matrix, by means of usual normalization rules (imposing a value of one to the r coefficients corresponding to the different dependent variables of long-run relationships) and zero exclusion restrictions.

Using these restrictions one can easily check that the α_0' matrix of structuralized long-run relationships is identified if we could impose r normalizing (value-one) non homogeneous restrictions (one for each row of the α_0' matrix, placed in different columns of the same matrix) and $r^2 - r$ exclusion restrictions, $r-1$ for each row of the α_0' matrix, arriving at a α_0' matrix with rank equal to r with probability one[7].

Once we have arrived at a unique, economically meaningful decomposition of the $A(1)$ matrix:

$$A(1) = \gamma_0 \, \alpha_0'$$

we can move onto the second stage devoted to the structuralization of instantaneous effects. For the K-model, in order to identify the K matrix we could use, alongside with other constraints, restrictions coming from the matrix of structuralized loadings[8]:

$$\gamma^* = K \gamma_0$$

The γ^* matrix of structuralized loadings could contain some zeros in correspondence to the equilibrium errors ($\alpha_0' \, y_{t-k}$) that, as economic theory suggests, are not to be loaded in the corresponding equations. These homogeneous restrictions, with the claim contained in the first paragraph of this section, could be easily accomodated with the usual formula:

$$R \, vecK = d$$

Once we have achieved identification, using information coming from F.I.M.L. cointegrating set-up, still trying to save the programs contained in Appendix D, we could

---

7 Incidentally, in order to identify (isolate) theoretically meaningful independent relationships, Johansen's (1989a,b) framework, dealing with restrictions on the cointegration space, could be used combined with considerations of the type made above in order to match situations where an overidentifying set-up is needed.

8 See Johansen (1989a,b) for the interpretation of the γ matrix as a matrix of loading coefficients.

use an unrestricted asymptotic least squares VAR in level set-up and usual formulae in order to find asymptotically correct distributions of impulse response functions.

7. The Working of an AB-Model

This section contains a discussion of how a Structural VAR model works on a real economic setting. To this end, I will qualitatively summarize some results of an exercise on Italian data (C. Giannini, A. Lanzarotti and M. Seghelini, "Traditional and Eclectic Interpretations of Macroeconomic Fluctuations: The Case of Italy", in preparation) which strictly parallels Blanchard's 1989 work on U.S. data.

The model considers the behaviour of five quarterly variables, namely: the logarithm of output (at constant prices), y; the unemployment rate, u; the logarithm of prices, p; the logarithm of nominal wages, w and the logarithm of nominal money, m. This latter variable is based upon the M2 aggregate, whereas Blanchard's work used the M1 aggregate.

Our usual y_t vector should be seen as

$$y'_t = \left[y_{1t}, y_{2t}, y_{3t}, y_{4t}, y_{5t}\right] = \left[y_t, u_t, p_t, w_t, m_t\right]$$

The traditional interpretation of macroeconomic fluctuations that, with some semantic qualms Blanchard call "Keynesian", relies a two-sided conceptual framework made of two blocks: aggregate demand and aggregate supply. Aggregate demand characterizes the behaviour of aggregate demand for goods given prices. Aggregate supply characterizes the behaviour of prices given output and include a relation between unemployment and output (Okun's law), a wage setting equation (the Phillips curve) and a price setting equation.

These relationships correspond to a system of five-equation connecting observable variables to unobservable independent shocks. This system will be presented later on.

Frequency domain techniques have been used to seasonally adjust the aforementioned variables referred to Italian data. Unit-root tests have then allowed us to qualify our seasonally adjusted series as $I(1)$ variables including Italy's unemployment rate[1].

---

1 This last result was in contrast with the empirical results of similar series referred to other countries. We have tried to correct this somewhat absurd result using a

Our estimation of the reduced form (an unstructured VAR model) provided another difference with Blanchard's analysis that, surprisingly enough, had found no evidence of cointegration between the variables referred to U.S. data.

We found strikingly different results on this point through the application of Johansen methodology.

Starting from a "reduced form" of the type

$$A(L)\, y_t = \mu + \varepsilon_t$$

$$A(0) = I_n$$

where μ is a vector of constant terms and using standard testing procedures (see Sims, Stock and Watson, 1990, p. 134) we have found a maximum lag length equal to 4. Then using Johansen's F.I.M.L. set-up we have unambiguously found a cointegrating rank (r) equal to 3, so the $A(1)$ matrix

$$A(1) = I - A_1 - A_2 - A_3 - A_4$$

can be factorized as

$$A(1) = \gamma\, \alpha'$$

with γ and α full column rank matrices of 5×3 order.

Using exclusion restrictions and usual normalization rules we have tried to isolate three theoretically meaningful independent cointegrating vectors corresponding to long-run relations between the variables. Such relations can fall within a "Keynesian"-like conceptual framework.

Using three normalizing non-homogeneous restrictions (one for each row of the α' matrix and each referred to different columns of the same matrix) and $r^2 - r$ (9-3) exclusion restrictions, r–1 (3-1) for each row of the α' matrix we arrived at the following structure[2]

---

corrected unemployment rate which accounts for the trending effect of the participation of Italian women to the labour market. However, the corrected series still behaved as a $I(1)$ process.

2 The signs and magnitudes of free α_{ij} coefficients of the α matrix looked economically correct.

$$\alpha' = \begin{bmatrix} \alpha_{11} & 0 & \alpha_{31} & 0 & 1 \\ 1 & \alpha_{22} & 0 & 0 & \alpha_{52} \\ 0 & 1 & \alpha_{33} & \alpha_{43} & 0 \end{bmatrix}$$

Remembering the ordering of the y_t vector ($y'_t = \left[y_t, u_t, p_t, w_t, m_t \right]$), the first row of the α' matrix corresponds to a quantitative theory of money equation, the second row corresponds to a long-run relation between output, the level of activity and money, stressing with this last variable the crucial role played by the Bank of Italy in controlling (also in the long run) real aggregates through monetary interventions; the third row corresponds to an augmented Phillips curve.

The z_t (3×1) vector ($z_t = \alpha' y_t$) of cointegration residuals could be interpreted as made up of three equilibrium errors as follows

$$z_t = \begin{bmatrix} z_{mt} \\ z_{yt} \\ z_{yt} \end{bmatrix}$$

The three elements correspond to monetary, real output and unemployment equilibrium errors respectively.

As already noted in section 6, a different parametrization could have been chosen to isolate theoretically meaningful independent relations and Johansen (1989a,b) set-up could be employed, if necessary, when overidentifying restrictions were needed to isolate theoretically meaningful equilibrium relations.

Having made our choice, the matrix of unstructured loadings γ, is completely numerically defined with every element γ_{ij} different from zero with probability one.

Let us now turn to the problem of structuralization of instantaneous correlations. Recalling the ordered content of y_t (and correspondingly of ε_t and e_t), five equations connecting reduced form innovations (ε_t) to structuralized shocks (e_t) can be obtained by closely following Blanchard's (1989, p. 1148) parametrizations.

AD - an aggregate demand equation

$$\varepsilon_{yt} = b_{12} e_{2t} + b_{11} e_{1t}$$

where innovations in real output ε_{yt} are attributed to demand e_{1t} and supply e_{2t} shocks.

OL - an Okun's law equation

$$\varepsilon_{ut} + a_{21}\varepsilon_{yt} = b_{22}e_{2t}$$

where innovations in the unemployment rate (ε_{ut}) are attributed, given output, to supply shocks (e_{2t}).

PS - a price-setting equation

$$\varepsilon_{pt} + a_{34}\varepsilon_{wt} + a_{31}\varepsilon_{yt} = b_{32}e_{2t} + b_{33}e_{3t}$$

where innovations in prices given wages and output are attributed to supply e_{2t} and price e_{3t} shocks.

WS - a wage-setting equation

$$\varepsilon_{wt} + a_{43}\varepsilon_{pt} + a_{42}\varepsilon_{ut} = b_{42}e_{2t} + b_{44}e_{45}$$

where innovations in wages given prices and unemployment are attributed to supply e_{2t} and wage e_{4t} shocks.

MR - a monetary rule equation

$$\varepsilon_{mt} - a_{51}\varepsilon_{yt} + a_{52}\varepsilon_{ut} + a_{53}\varepsilon_{pt} + a_{54}\varepsilon_{wt} = b_{55}e_{5t}$$

where innovations in nominal money (ε_{mt}) given real output, unemployment, prices and wages are attributed to money shocks. (See Blanchard 1989 for a thorough economic discussion of the equations.)

Under these hypotheses, our AB-model will have the following A and B matrices

$$A = \begin{bmatrix} 1 & 0 & 0 & 0 & 0 \\ a_{21} & 1 & 0 & 0 & 0 \\ a_{31} & 0 & 1 & a_{34} & 0 \\ 0 & a_{42} & a_{43} & 1 & 0 \\ a_{51} & a_{52} & a_{53} & a_{54} & 1 \end{bmatrix}$$

$$B = \begin{bmatrix} b_{11} & b_{12} & 0 & 0 & 0 \\ 0 & b_{22} & 0 & 0 & 0 \\ 0 & b_{32} & b_{33} & 0 & 0 \\ 0 & b_{42} & 0 & b_{44} & 0 \\ 0 & 0 & 0 & 0 & b_{55} \end{bmatrix}$$

The two matrices have 17 free elements, this means that the necessary (order) conditions for identification have been violated. In fact there are two elements too many since the estimated $(\hat{\Sigma})$ variance-covariance matrix of unstructured VAR model disturbances contained only 15 different elements.

In his aforementioned work, Blanchard obtained exact identification by assigning fixed numerical values to coefficients a_{34} and b_{12}; the first came from an earlier study while the second resulted from a sort of calibration reasoning.

We have followed a different route.

Firstly, we have set the value of coefficient a_{43} in equation WS to 0 considering that price changes can hardly cause "instantaneous" wage movements over three months. In Sims' (1988) terminology, this would be a "minimum delay" restriction.

Secondly, we have imposed a restriction on the structuralized matrix of loadings. In a Johansen-like parametrization, we can go from

$$A(L)\, y_t = \mu + \varepsilon_t$$

$$A(1) = \gamma\, \alpha'$$

to the following equivalent equations

$$A^*(L)\, \Delta y_t = \mu - A(1)\, y_{t-4} + \varepsilon_t \qquad A^*(0) = I_5$$

$$A^*(L)\, \Delta y_t = \mu - (\gamma\alpha')\, y_{t-4} + \varepsilon_t$$

Then, taking into account that $\alpha' y_{t-4} = z_{t-4}$, we can arrive at

$$A^*(L)\,\Delta y_t = \mu - \gamma z_{t-4} + \varepsilon_t$$

The γ loading matrix applies to the z_{t-4} vector which contains the equilibrium errors mentioned above.

$$z'_{t-4} = \left[z_{mt-4},\ z_{yt-4},\ z_{ut-4} \right]$$

In this way - i.e. premultiplication by the A matrix - the nucleus γz_{t-4} of a Johansen-like parametrization after structuralization becomes

$$A\gamma z_{t-4} = \gamma^* z_{t-4}$$

At this point, we inserted a constraint on the structuralized matrix of loadings in the following way

$$A\gamma = \gamma^* = \begin{bmatrix} * * * \\ 0 * * \\ * * * \\ * * * \\ * * * \end{bmatrix}$$

where asterisks inside matrices stand for free values.

In this way[3], the structured loading matrix γ^* says that, within the structured VAR model, the monetary equilibrium error does not affect the equation which explains unemployment changes.

We have thus obtained exact identification (necessary and sufficient conditions for identification put forward in this monograph have been obviously checked) so we could begin estimation.

Looking at estimation results, we found that all coefficients, save a_{51}, were significantly different from 0 at a 5% significance level. We therefore dropped coefficient a_{51} and moved from exact identification to overidentification.

---

3 From an analytical point of view, the constraint we are dealing with implies that the inner product of the second row of the A matrix and the first column of the γ matrix is equal to zero.

We then re-estimated the model without coefficient a_{51} and found that all parameters were significantly different from 0, had the expected signs and were of reasonable magnitude. We then tried to insert other restrictions on the structured loading matrix but they were all forcefully rejected by the data after performing the overidentifying restriction test.

Incidentally, I would like to point out that the attempt to impose restrictions on the loading matrix and strongly sparse structures on matrices A and B may give rise to conflicts. Sometimes such restrictions could lead to a system of inconsistent constraints.

Assuming the aforementioned model as valid, we then moved to the dynamic simulation step. We have calculated twenty-five impulse response functions (one for each variable and for each shock) and twenty-five forecast error variance decomposition functions together with the associated confidence bounds. In the interpretation of these functions I will focus on the main differences and similarities with respect to the results obtained by O.J. Blanchard on U.S. data.

Following Blanchard, let us start with FEVD functions.

Figures 1 to 5 of table 1 show portions of the forecast error variance of the variables due to each structural innovation in relation to Italian data. Our results parallel O.J. Blanchard findings in attributing a dominant role to real innovations to explain fluctuations of real variables. A remarkable difference is that innovations in nominal variables replace the dominant role attributed by Blanchard to supply innovations in explaining output fluctuations in the medium and long-run.

The last one seems to be a strong feature of our exercise on Italian data strengthened by the fact that our FEVD functions are much more tightly distributed than Blanchard's.

Some important considerations can be drawn for Italian economy looking at FEVD functions for the nominal variables. In particular, wages typically behave as an exogenous variable being at any horizon substantially unaffected by other innovations.

Innovations in wages instead, greatly influence, with an increasing effect over time, prices and money movements. This is a crucial but largely expected feature of Italian economy, one that is strongly consistent with the central role attributed to labour costs.

Table 2 contains the plots of a selected set of impulse response functions, together with the associated one-standard-deviation confidence bounds.

One can see that output innovations induce usual short-run reactions in real variables, output and unemployment, followed by more rapid and stronger (with respect to Blanchard findings) opposite movements. This may be understood considering the particularly open nature of the Italian economy, the perverse effect of output growth on the Italian balance of payments and the corresponding reaction of the monetary authority.

Nominal variables' responses to output innovations (not reported) show, after few quarters, wide confidence bounds making it hard to draw any robust conclusion. Similar results stem from the analysis of responses to unemployment shocks.

While in Blanchard both prices and wages innovations have surprisingly short-run positive effects on real variables, in our findings prices innovations decrease output and increase unemployment, and wages innovations have a short-run positive demand effect vanishing after one year in correspondence of the full adjustment of prices in response to the same shock (see figures 4, 5 and 6 of table 2).

Like Blanchard results, money innovations seem to have expansive effects on the real economy, but looking at output and unemployment FEVD functions (see table 1), the role played by monetary shocks is negligible.

Concluding this brief description of our results, one could argue that simulation evidence looks composite. In accordance with Blanchard findings one can assert that in the Italian economy, demand shocks look the pre-eminent cause of fluctuations in real variables, at least in the short run. In contrast with Blanchard results on the U.S. economy, supply shocks play a marginal role in the movement of real variables not only in the short run but also in the long run.

O.J. Blanchard's 1989 paper does not report FEVD functions for the nominal variables. Looking at our results, something surprising seems to be in contrast with a Keynesian interpretation of prices and wages fluctuations. In fact, these variables (prices and wages), though sticky in the short run (practically by assumption), do not move after some periods to balance the effects of real shocks. In our exercise, looking at the corresponding FEVD functions, the fluctuations in nominal variables are almost entirely explained by their own shocks at any horizon.

Table I:

Portion of Forecast Error Variance Decompositions due to innovations in:

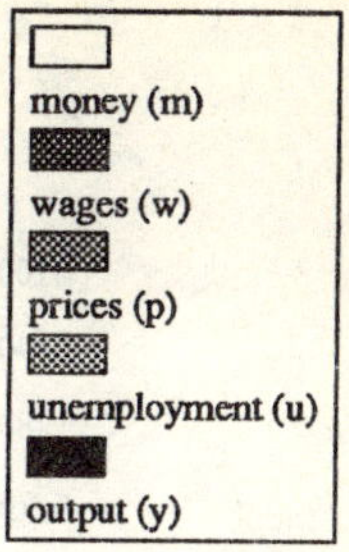

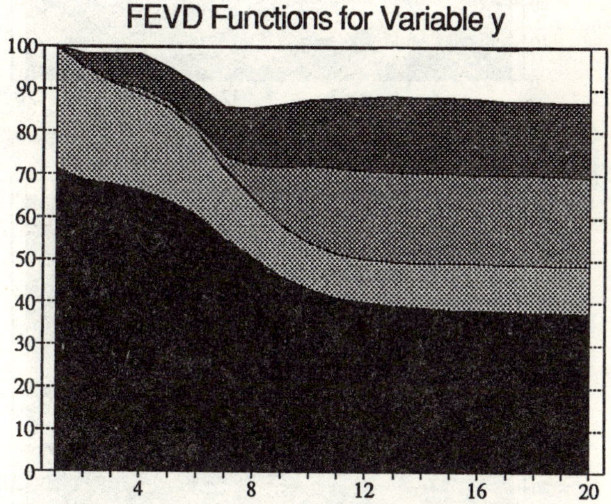

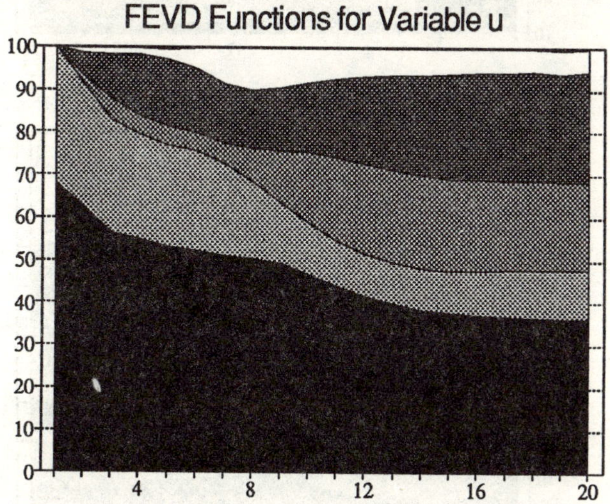

Table I (continued)

FEVD Functions for Variable p

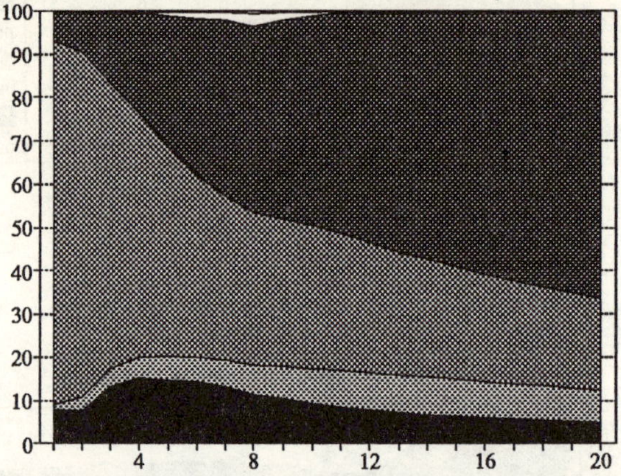

FEVD Functions for Variable w

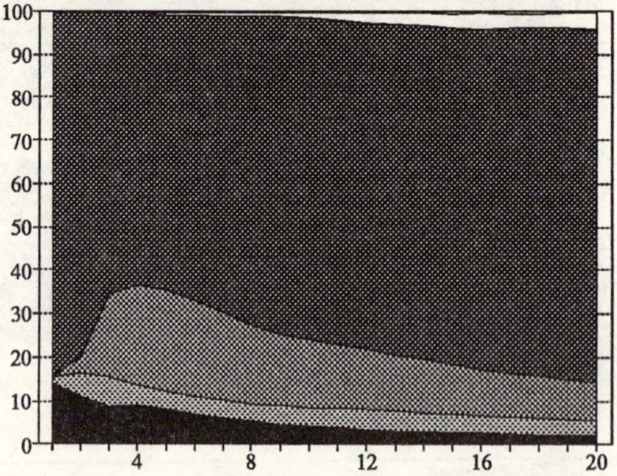

FEVD Functions for Variable m

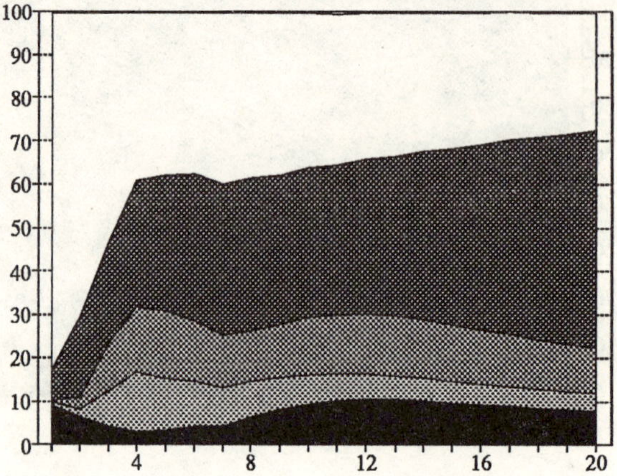

Table II

Impulse Response Functions

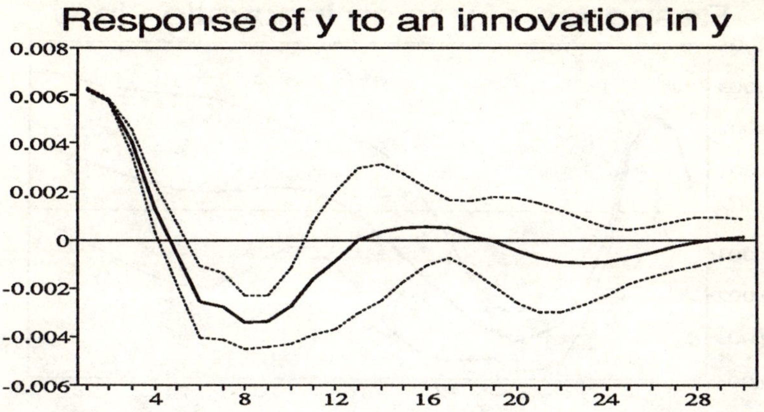

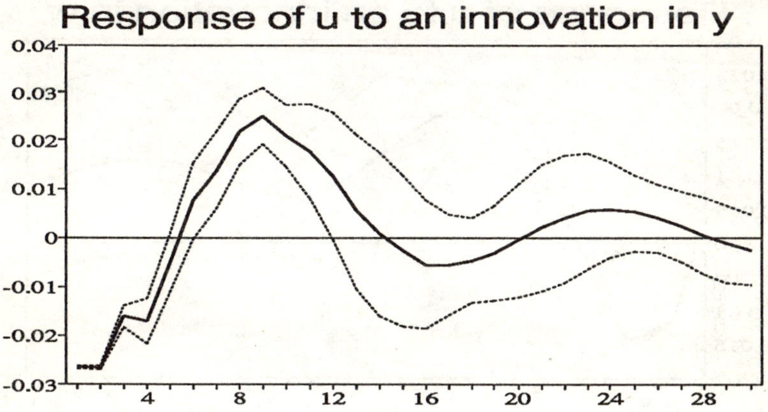

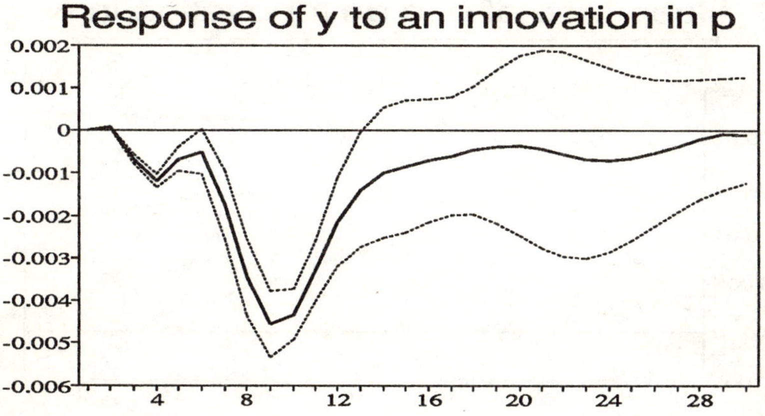

Table II

(continued)

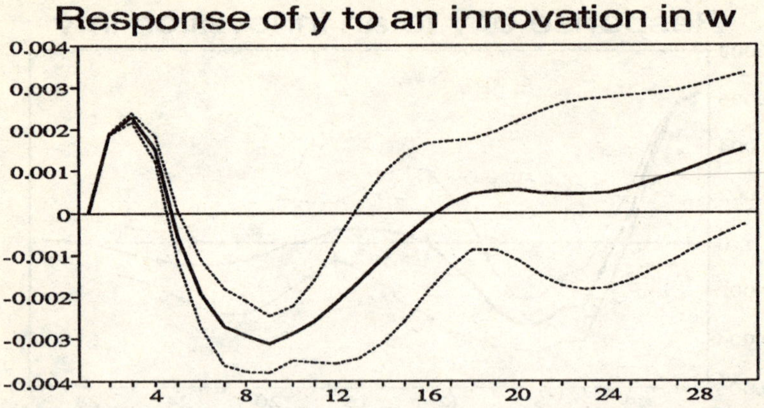

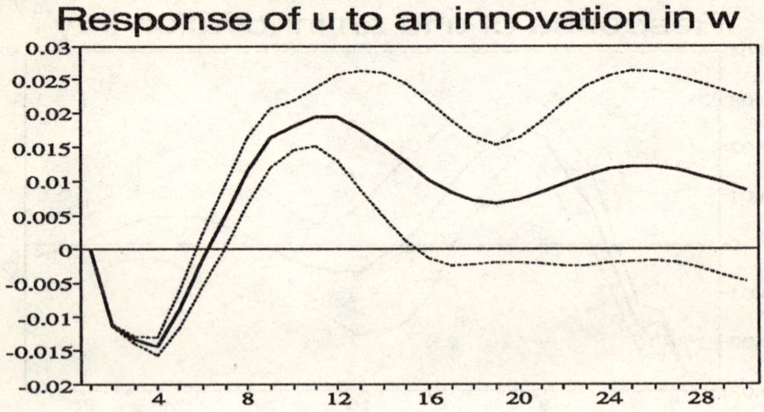

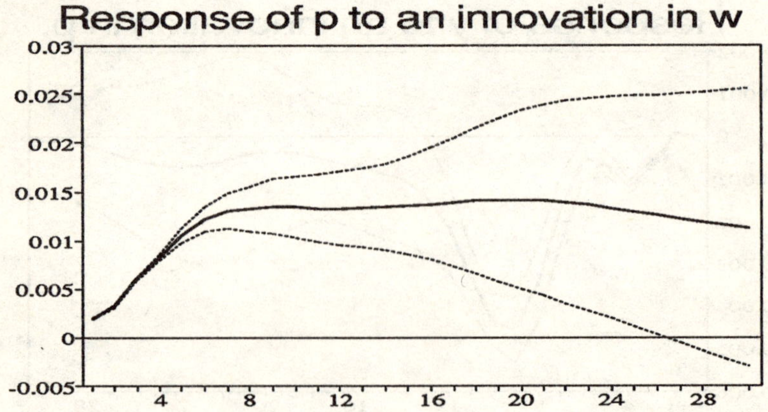

ANNEX 1: The Notions of Reduced Form and Structure in Structural VAR Modeling

Following Sims (1986) the present Annex attempts to illustrate the particular notion of structure in Structural VAR Analysis. The notions of structure, identification and reduced form are deeply connected in any econometric approach. In Structural VAR Analysis the reduced form of a vector y_t of economic variables is simply represented by a vector autoregression of the type:

$$A(L)\, y_t = \varepsilon_t$$

$$A(L) = I - A_1 L \ldots A_p L^p$$

and ε_t is a vector normal white noise with

$$E(\varepsilon_t\, \varepsilon'_t) = \Sigma.$$

The first stage of Structural VAR Analysis is the estimation of the reduced form.

At this stage one can impose no theoretical a-priori constraint (apart from the number and type of economic variables included in the y_t vector). Thus unconstrained VAR Analysis can be seen as nothing more than a convenient way of organizing the correlations between the variables of interest.

There is no reason to leave the first stage at this level of generality. For example, think of the problem of non-stationarity and cointegration. Cointegration is a property of the data and if the so-called "cointegration space" is not subject to structural interpretation, cointegration pertains only to statistics, not to economic theory.

Inserting cointegration constraints in a VAR in levels is only a way to arrive at a reduced form that "better" summarizes the correlations between the variables under study ("better" should be understood as "more efficiently").

In the first stage of Structural VAR Analysis one may decide to move further on: the notion of non-causality, obviously unlike the problem of imposing direction to instantaneous causality, is still a property, concerning subsets of variables in y_t, which may be detected on the basis of reduced form estimation. In this sense non-causality (as was the case for cointegration) is a property of the data and not of any economic theoretical model. In the first stage then, non-causality restrictions can be used to arrive at reduced forms that "better" summarize the correlation between variables. Obviously, a number of other considerations should be used to extend the restrictions on the reduced form in the first stage and find more efficient reduced form representations.

Let us assume for simplicity that the first stage of Structural VAR Analysis could end with an estimate of the parameters of an unrestricted reduced form

$$A(L)\, y_t = \varepsilon_t \qquad E(\varepsilon_t\, \varepsilon'_t) = \Sigma$$

obtaining estimates of $A_1 \ldots A_p$ as $\hat{A}_1 \ldots \hat{A}_p$

$$\hat{\varepsilon}_t = \hat{A}(L)\, y_t$$

$$\hat{\Sigma} = \sum_{t=1}^{T} \frac{\hat{\varepsilon}_t\, \hat{\varepsilon}'_t}{T}$$

In VAR Analysis the only source of variation of y_t variables (apart from hypothetical changes in initial conditions or changes in a vector of deterministic part) are random shocks that in the reduced form are represented by the vector white noise ε_t.

The vector of unobservable ε_t variables, often called vector of innovations or vector of surprise variables, can also be seen as the vector of unexplained random variations obtained as a residual from the projection of y_t vector over its possibly infinite past (truncated at p by virtue of plausible approximation rules).

In the ε_t vector of unobservable variables one can expect a substantial amount of contemporaneous correlation - not necessarily due to problems connected to temporal aggregation - which gives rise to a "theoretical" variance covariance matrix of ε_t, Σ, typically not diagonal.

Structural VAR Analysis focuses its structural effort onto the organization of istanteneous correlation between innovation variables.

In the most general model studied in this monograph (the AB-model) the ε_t vector must satisfy the following set of conditions:

$A\,\varepsilon_t = B e_t$ — A and B invertible matrices of order n

$E(e_t) = [0]$ — $E(e_t\, e'_t) = I_n$

so

$$A\,\Sigma\, A' = B\, B'$$

The vector of e_t variables is a vector of orthonormal random variables whose components are equal in number and corresponding in content to the list of variables contained in the y_t vector and can be thought as independent unit variance random shocks of the corresponding y_{it} variables.

These independent unit variance random shocks can be considered the ultimate independent source of variation of y_t variables in time.

With the information contained in the estimated variance covariance matrix of the unrestricted reduced form, $\hat{\Sigma}$, and an appropriate number (and form) of a-priori restrictions on matrices A and B (together with some normalization restrictions) one can presumably arrive at the conditions for unique identification of the A and B matrices.

In this case the structural form of the VAR model becomes

$$A^*(L)\, y_t = B\, e_t$$

where

$$A^*(L) = A\, A(L)$$

This structural form, on the basis of its parameters (once estimated), can be used to examine the path of estimated effects of (unit) changes (shocks) in the vector e_t of independent zero mean variables.

In the words of Hurwicz (1962) the equation

$$A^*(L)\, y_t = B\, e_t$$

is in structural form with respect to modifications of e_t.

Obviously this structural form has behavioural content if the *A* and *B* matrices contain the supposed "true" agent's behaviour in response to modifications of the e_t vector.

ANNEX 2: Some Considerations on the Semantics, Choice and Management of the K, C and AB-Models

This annex is devoted to illustrating my point of view on the significance of each type of model in relation with its corresponding set of identifying restrictions. The discussion may shed new light on the problem of which model to choose for specific applications. The present annex also includes some considerations on the "overall" working of the three models.

One point may need to be clarified beforehand, though. The AB-model, the most general of the three, may be cast in a K-model form by writing

$$K = B^{-1} A$$

or in a C-model form by writing

$$C = A^{-1} B$$

Moreover, the K-model could be seen as a C-model (and vice-versa) if one noted that

$$K = C^{-1}, \qquad C = K^{-1}$$

I will call "genuine" K, C and AB models, the models which allow us to reach identification through a set of <u>linear</u> constraints of the type

$$R_k \, vec\, K = d_k$$

$$R_c \, vec\, C = d_c$$

$$\begin{cases} R_a \, vec\, A = d_a \\ R_b \, vec\, B = d_b \end{cases}$$

respectively.

The transformation of "genuine" K, C or AB-models into models of the C and K type in general give rise to a set of very complicated non-linear restrictions with respect to the coefficients of the C and K matrices of the transformed models.

Such restrictions can not be dealt with within the framework put forward in the present monograph; therefore only "genuine" models can be discussed in the set-up I propose.

Looking at the different models and starting from the autoregressive representation of the so-called first stage

$$A(L)\, y_t = \varepsilon_t$$

$$A(0) = I_n$$

$$E(\varepsilon_t\, \varepsilon_t') = \Sigma$$

matrices K, C and A and B operate in the following way within the above-mentioned system

$$K\, A(L)\, y_t = e_t \quad \text{for the K-model}$$

$$A(L)\, y_t = C\, e_t \quad \text{for the C-model}$$

$$A\, A(L)\, y_t = B\, e_t \quad \text{for the AB-model}$$

with $E(e_t\, e_t') = I_n$

In the K-model, matrix K directly applies to vector y_t of observable quantities. Instantaneous correlations between observable variables are organized through the structure of the K matrix. On the contrary, instantaneous correlations between the unobservable quantities contained in the e_t shocks vector can in no way be directly organized in the K-model.

In the C-model, matrix C directly applies to vector e_t of unobservable quantities. Instantaneous co-movements of y_t observable variables are indirectly organized since they result as linear combinations of a vector of independent shocks. Instantaneous co-movements of observable variables contained in the y_t vector can in no way be directly organized in the C-model.

In the AB-model, matrices A and B apply to observable and unobservable quantities respectively. Thus the gratest flexibility is assured.

In order to tackle the problem of which choice between models in concrete applications, the first question the researcher must solve is whether the concrete problem under study admits a plausible formulation in terms of "genuine" K, C, or AB models as defined in this annex.

The K-model is central in this monograph almost exclusively for analytical purposes. It could be better understood when regarded as the result of the transformation of a particular AB-model with ones on the A matrix main diagonal and (positive) elements only on the B matrix diagonal. In this way, also the K matrix

$$K = B^{-1} A$$

would have positive diagonal elements and exclusion restrictions on the coefficients of matrix A (ie., zero values for the corresponding elements) would not change their positions in the K matrix.

In the K-model, apart from restrictions imposed on the positive diagonal (K_{ii}) elements, the presence of a K_{ij} $(i \neq j)$ coefficient different from zero results from a combination of theoretical and commonsense considerations.

Every economic theory generally assumes the so-called "logical time" but in our context we will consider real time. Thus causal relationships derived from economic theory (eg. a causal relation linking variable j to variable i) can hold "instantaneously" only if they operate in the sampling period we are dealing with.

In other words, taking into account what Sims (1988) calls "minimum delay restrictions", a "logical-time" causal relation is a necessary but not sufficient conditions for the corresponding K_{ij} coefficient to be different from zero.

In general, using the K-model and looking at an unchanged set of variables, one can expect that the progressive shortening the sample period produces a corresponding progressive deletion of extradiagonal elements of the K matrix.

The K-model turns out to be particularly useful if economic theory can provide the researcher with some indication on the magnitudes of some total multipliers on observable variables. In this way, the considerations contained in the first paragraph of section 6 could be used to achieve identification.

At first glance, the C-model looks less appealing as regards theoretical and common-sense justifications of the organization of observable variables' co-movements. In fact, C-models look particularly useful when long-run constraints have to be imposed (such as neutrality conditions), often supposed to be valid in some actual economic contexts. For example, suppose that vector y_t is obtained by differentiating a vector (x_t) of I(1) non-cointegrated variables and possessing the usual (stable) autoregressive representation

$$A(L)\, y_t = \varepsilon_t$$

$$A(L)\, \Delta x_t = \varepsilon_t$$

The stable $A(L)$ polynomial matrix can be inverted so to move to the equivalent Wold representation

$$\Delta x_t = C(L)\, \varepsilon_t$$

Taking into account that in the C-model

$$\varepsilon_t = C\, e_t$$

we can write

$$\Delta x_t = C(L)\, C\, e_t$$

where vector e_t should contain shocks which are similar in nature and ordering to the elements of the Δx_t vector.

In order to identify C in a "genuine" C-model set-up, apart from a number of zero constraints on the C-matrix off-diagonal elements, we might impose some long-run restrictions derived from the analysis of

$$C^*(1) = C(1)\, C$$

where $C^*(1)$ is the matrix containing the "structured" multipliers of the elements of the e_t shocks vector in relation to the elements of the Δx_t vector.

Let us suppose we wanted to impose a neutrality constraint such as the following: the level of the i variable remain unchanged in the long run in response to movements of the j variable. In this case, we should only constrain to zero the $c^*_{ij}(1)$ element of the C^*_{ij} matrix, which is tantamount to say that an independent shock to the j variable has a zero total effect on the change of the i variable. As a consequence, integrating the difference, we could see that a shock in the j variable does not affect the level of the i variable. These and other long-run restrictions could easily be accommodated in our "genuine" C-model with constraints of the form

$$R_C \, vec \, C = d_C$$

(see, for example, Shapiro and Watson 1988 and Blanchard and Quah 1989 for the use of C-models with constraints of this type.)

The AB-model's characteristic flexibility makes it the most promising candidate in a number of applications, with a warning. The aforementioned long-run restrictions put on models K and C cannot be incorporated into a "genuine" AB-model because they correspond to complex non-linear constraints in the AB-model.

In section 7, a way to tackle a cointegrated set-up in the AB-model is discussed in some detail.

However, one should not forget that achieving identification of K, C and AB models is only the first step in Structural VAR model analysis.

The second step consists in estimating the parameters of the chosen "genuine" model. After estimation, one should first check that all estimated parameters are statistically significant and, if this is the case, that their signs and magnitudes are economically plausible. Moreover, in the case of overidentification, one should make sure that overidentifying restrictions are accepted by the data.

If estimation produces satisfactory results, the final step is dynamic simulation analysis carried out with instruments such as impulse response analysis and forecast error variance decomposition analysis. Only at this step can one fully appreciate the overall working of a Structural VAR model.

Not surprisingly, this last step can produce strikingly contrasting results, especially as regards the congruence of the economic theory subsumed in the identification step and, at times, from the point of view of sound economic judgement.

This situation can indeed arise looking at the fact that unstructured VAR modelling (representing the first stage of Structural VAR strategy) is independent from prejudices or supposedly "true" economic knowledge used in the identification step of the "genuine" K, C or AB-model chosen.

In SVAR dynamic simulation analysis a somehow arbitrary theoretical structure has to be combined with a plausibly "true" model of the data: their mix does not necessarily make a good-tasting cake.

In this case, a researcher must go back to the first step and look for more plausible "genuine" models. From a statistical point of view, the problem of choice between alternative structuralizations of the <u>same</u> unstructured VAR model - in line with the suggestions contained in the Foreword - can reasonably be posed only for models that yield satisfactory results after the third step has been carried out.

APPENDIX A

Matrix differentiation: first derivative

Let $f = (f_1, \dots f_m)'$ be a vector function with values in R^m which is differentiable on a set S of values in R^n. Let

$$\frac{\partial f_i(x)}{\partial x_j}$$

denote the partial derivative of f_i with respect to the j-th variable. Then the $m \times n$ matrix

$$\begin{bmatrix} \frac{\partial f_1(x)}{\partial x_1} & \cdots & \frac{\partial f_1(x)}{\partial x_n} \\ \cdots & & \cdots \\ \frac{\partial f_m(x)}{\partial x_{11}} & \cdots & \frac{\partial f_m(x)}{\partial x_n} \end{bmatrix}$$

is called the derivative or the Jacobian matrix of $f(x)$ and is denoted as

$$\frac{\partial f(x)}{\partial x}$$

On the basis of the preceding definitions, the following rules will hold

a) if
$$\underset{(1\times 1)}{f(x)} = a'x = \sum_{i=1}^{n} a_i x_i$$

then
$$\frac{\partial f(x)}{\partial x} = \underset{(1\times n)}{a'}$$

b) if
$$\underset{(m\times 1)}{f(x)} = \underset{m\times n}{A}x = y$$

then
$$\frac{\partial f(x)}{\partial x} = A$$

c) if $\qquad Y = AXB,\ vecY = y$ and $vecX = x$

then $y = vec(AXB) = (B' \otimes A)\ vecX = (B' \otimes A)\ x$

so $\dfrac{\partial y}{\partial x} = (B' \otimes A)$

d) $\qquad \underset{(n \times n)}{vec\ X} = \textcircled{T}\ vecX'$

$\textcircled{T}$ is a $n^2 \times n^2$ matrix

$$\frac{\partial\ vecX}{\partial\ vecX'} = \textcircled{T}$$

$$\textcircled{T}^2 = I_{n^2} \qquad \textcircled{T}' = \textcircled{T} = \textcircled{T}^{-1}$$

(See Pollock 1979, p. 72)

e) if $\qquad Y = X^{-1}$

taking differentials (see Magnus and Neudecker 1988)

$$dY = -X^{-1}\,(dX)\,X^{-1}$$

and vectorizing

$$vec\ dY = -(X'^{-1} \otimes X^{-1})\ vec\ dX$$

$$\frac{\partial\ vecY}{\partial\ vecX} = -(X'^{-1} \otimes X^{-1})$$

f) Chain rule (Pollock 1979)

If $u = u(y)$ is a vector function of y and $y = y(x)$ is a function of vector x, so that $u = u\,[y(x)]$, then

$$\frac{\partial u}{\partial x} = \frac{\partial u}{\partial y} \cdot \frac{\partial y}{\partial x}$$

Matrix differentiation: second derivatives

(Magnus 1988)

Let $f(x): S \to R$ be a real-valued function defined and twice differentiable on a set S in R^n.

Let $\partial^2 f(x)/\partial x_i \partial x_j$ denote the second order partial derivative of $f(x)$ with respect to the i-th and j-th variables. Then the $n \times n$ matrix

$$\left\{ \frac{\partial^2 f(x)}{\partial x_i \partial x_j} \right\}$$

is called the Hessian matrix of $f(x)$ and is denoted as $H\,[f(x)]$ or

$$\frac{\partial^2 f(x)}{\partial x \partial x'}$$

following Dhrymes (1978), Pollock (1979) the Hessian matrix can be obtained as

$$\frac{\partial^2 f(x)}{\partial x \partial x'} = \frac{\partial}{\partial x} \left[\frac{\partial f(x)}{\partial x} \right]'$$

where

$$\left[\frac{\partial f(x)}{\partial x} \right]' = \frac{\partial f(x)}{\partial x'}$$

APPENDIX B

In this appendix, strictly following the notation and rules used in Pollock (1979, pp. 62-82) and Dhrymes (1978) we will calculate the first order conditions for the maximization of the likelihood function of the K model and the corresponding Hessian matrix.

Let us start from the log-likelihood

$$\mathcal{L} = c - \frac{T}{2}\log|\Sigma| - \frac{T}{2}\,tr(\Sigma^{-1}\hat{\Sigma})$$

where

$$K\,\Sigma\,K' = I_n,$$

assuming det $K \neq 0$, $\Sigma = (K'K)^{-1}$, and $R\ vecK = d$, or $vecK = S\gamma + s$

Substituting $\Sigma = (K'K)^{-1}$ in the log-likelihood we immediately arrive at

$$\mathcal{L} = c + T\log|K| - \frac{T}{2}\,tr(K'K\,\hat{\Sigma})$$

Using Pollock's (1979) notation

$$(K)^r = [vec(K')]'$$

and using Pollock's (1979, pp. 81-82) rules, we can write

$$\frac{\partial\mathcal{L}}{\partial\,vecK} = T(K^{-1})^r - T\,(vecK)'\,(\hat{\Sigma}\otimes I)$$

using the chain rule of matrix differentiation

$$\frac{\partial\mathcal{L}}{\partial\gamma} = \frac{\partial\mathcal{L}}{\partial\,vecK}\cdot\frac{\partial\,vecK}{\partial\gamma} = \frac{\partial\mathcal{L}}{\partial\,vecK}S$$

Then the first order conditions for the maximization of the log-likelihood are respectively for $vecK$ and γ

$$T(K^{-1})^r - T(vecK)'(\hat{\Sigma}\otimes I) = \underset{n^2\times 1}{[0]}$$

$$\left[T(K^{-1})^r - T(vecK)'(\hat{\Sigma}\otimes I)\right]S = \underset{l\times 1}{[0]}$$

Now, on the basis of the obtained formula for the gradient vector, we can calculate the corresponding Hessian matrices:

(a) $$\frac{\partial^2 \mathcal{L}}{\partial\, vecK\, \partial\, vecK'}$$

(b) $$\frac{\partial^2 \mathcal{L}}{\partial \gamma \partial \gamma'}$$

remembering that on the basis of the definition of K^r

$$(K^{-1})^r = \left\{vec\left[(K^{-1})'\right]\right\}'$$

the gradient vector

$$\frac{\partial \mathcal{L}}{\partial\, vecK}$$

can be rewritten in the following way

$$\frac{\partial \mathcal{L}}{\partial\, vecK} = T\left\{vec\left[(K^{-1})'\right]\right\}' - T(vecK)'(\hat{\Sigma}\otimes I)$$

Following Dhrymes (1978) we can calculate the Hessian matrix as

$$H(vecK) = \frac{\partial^2 \mathcal{L}}{\partial\, vecK\, \partial\, vec(K')} = \frac{\partial}{\partial\, vecK}\left(\frac{\partial \mathcal{L}}{\partial\, vecK}\right)' = \frac{\partial}{\partial\, vecK}\left(\frac{\partial \mathcal{L}}{\partial\, (vecK)'}\right)$$

$$\frac{\partial \mathcal{L}}{\partial\, vec(K')} = T\, vec(K'^{-1}) - T(\hat{\Sigma}\otimes I)(vecK)$$

and then

$$H(vecK) = \frac{\partial^2 \mathcal{L}}{\partial\, vecK\, \partial\, vec(K')} = T\frac{\partial\, vec(K^{-1\prime})}{\partial\, vecK} - T(\hat{\Sigma}\otimes I)$$

Let us concentrate on the first member of the last expression. Using the chain rule we can write

$$\frac{\partial\, vec(K'^{-1})}{\partial\, vecK} = \frac{\partial\, vec(K'^{-1})}{\partial\, vec(K')} \cdot \frac{\partial\, vec(K')}{\partial\, vecK}$$

Using the rules introduced in Appendix A (see Pollock 1979, p. 81) we can write

$$\frac{\partial\, vec(K'^{-1})}{\partial\, vecK} = -\left[K^{-1} \otimes (K')^{-1}\right] \cdot Ⓣ$$

so we can arrive at

$$H(vecK) = \frac{\partial^2 \mathcal{L}}{\partial\, vecK\, \partial\, vecK'} = -T\left\{\left[K^{-1} \otimes (K')^{-1}\right] Ⓣ + (\hat{\Sigma} \otimes I)\right\}$$

Remembering that $vecK = S\gamma + s$ is an affine function (see Theorem 11 in Magnus and Neudecker 1988, p. 112), the following Hessian matrix is simply

$$H(\gamma) = \frac{\partial^2 \mathcal{L}}{\partial\gamma\, \partial\gamma'} = S'\, H(vecK)\, S$$

APPENDIX C

by Antonio Lanzarotti and Mario Seghelini

This appendix is devoted to the symbolic identification analysis of some potentially interesting examples for the K, C and AB-models.

Its main purpose is to show the practical working of the identification conditions developed in this monograph, doing it by means of some particular features of the models considered.

For the first example we will present the calculations in more detail, while for the other we will skip some obvious passages.

K-model

Remembering condition b) at page 19, the model is locally identified if and only if the system

$$R_k \,(K' \otimes I)\, \widetilde{D}_n \, x = [0]$$

has the unique admissible solution $x = [0]$.

<u>EXAMPLE 1</u>

We focus our attention on the K-model considered in Bekker and Pollock (1986). The K matrix takes the form:

$$K = \begin{bmatrix} k_{11} & 0 & k_{13} \\ k_{21} & k_{22} & 0 \\ 0 & k_{32} & k_{33} \end{bmatrix}$$

obtained imposing the homogeneous constraints: $k_{12}=k_{23}=k_{31}=0$.

The R_k matrix thus can be:

$$R_k=\begin{bmatrix} 000100000 \\ 000000010 \\ 001000000 \end{bmatrix}$$

and the D_n matrix, following Magnus (1988), can take the form:

$$\tilde{D}_n=\begin{bmatrix} 0 & 0 & 0 \\ 1 & 0 & 0 \\ 0 & 1 & 0 \\ -1 & 0 & 0 \\ 0 & 0 & 0 \\ 0 & 0 & 1 \\ 0 & -1 & 0 \\ 0 & 0 & -1 \\ 0 & 0 & 0 \end{bmatrix}$$

Simple calculations yield:

$$R_k(K'\otimes I)\,\tilde{D}_n=\begin{bmatrix} -k_{22} & -k_{32} & 0 \\ k_{13} & 0 & -k_{33} \\ 0 & k_{11} & k_{21} \end{bmatrix}$$

Now we have to solve the system:

$$\begin{bmatrix} -k_{22} & -k_{32} & 0 \\ k_{13} & 0 & -k_{33} \\ 0 & k_{11} & k_{21} \end{bmatrix}\cdot\begin{bmatrix} x_1 \\ x_2 \\ x_3 \end{bmatrix}=[0]$$

Noting that matrix:

$$R_k(K'\otimes I)\,\tilde{D}_n$$

has determinant diferent from zero with probability one, it is easy to demonstrate that the aforementioned system has the unique solution $x_1=x_2=x_3=0$.

The model is just identified (the number of contraints being equal to $n(n-1)/2$).

EXAMPLE 2

This example aims to show that a number of constraints greater than $n(n-1)/2$ does not necessarly implies the over-identification of a model; in certain situations, also the constraint form plays an important role.

Let us consider a bivariate K-model with the constraints: $k_{21} = -k_{12}$;

the K matrix, then, takes the following form:

$$K = \begin{bmatrix} k_{11} & -k_{21} \\ k_{21} & k_{22} \end{bmatrix}$$

and a possible form of R_k is:

$$R_k = [0\ 1\ 1\ 0]$$

It is easy to show, following the same steps as in the previous example, that this model is just identified: in fact

$$x_1\,(-k_{11} + k_{22}) = 0$$

has the unique solution $x_1 = 0$. If we go further, adding the constraint $k_{11} = k_{22}$, the model becomes unidentified. In fact with:

$$K = \begin{bmatrix} k_{11} & -k_{21} \\ k_{21} & k_{11} \end{bmatrix} \text{ and } R_k = \begin{bmatrix} 0 & 1 & 1 & 0 \\ 1 & 0 & 0 & -1 \end{bmatrix}$$

we get

$$R_k\,(K' \otimes I)\,\tilde{D}_n = [0]$$

Now

$$\begin{bmatrix} 0 \\ 0 \end{bmatrix} x_1 = [0]$$

has solution for every x_1.

C-model

According to condition b) at page 28, we get identification of a C-model if the system

$$R_c\,(I\otimes C)\,\tilde{D}_n\cdot x=[0]$$

has the unique admissible solution $x=[0]$.

EXAMPLE 3

In this model we impose three homogeneous constraints, $c_{12}=c_{13}=c_{31}=0$, together with the additional constraint $c_{32}=c_{23}$, so the C-matrix becomes:

$$C=\begin{bmatrix} c_{11} & 0 & 0 \\ c_{21} & c_{22} & c_{23} \\ 0 & c_{23} & c_{33} \end{bmatrix}$$

and a possible R_c is:

$$R_c=\begin{bmatrix} 0&0&1&0&0&0&0&0&0 \\ 0&0&0&1&0&0&0&0&0 \\ 0&0&0&0&0&1&0&-1&0 \\ 0&0&0&0&0&0&1&0&0 \end{bmatrix}$$

Simple calculations give us the following system:

$$\begin{bmatrix} c_{23} & c_{33} & 0 \\ -c_{11} & 0 & 0 \\ 0 & c_{21} & (c_{33}+c_{22}) \\ 0 & -c_{11} & 0 \end{bmatrix}\cdot\begin{bmatrix} x_1 \\ x_2 \\ x_3 \end{bmatrix}=0$$

whose unique solution is given by $x_1=x_2=x_3=0$.

The model is identified, i.e. generally over-identified, the number of constraints being greater than $n(n-1)/2$.

EXAMPLE 4

Now, let us consider a model derived from a block diagonal structure. The C-matrix takes the form:

$$C=\begin{bmatrix} c_{11} & 0 & c_{13} \\ 0 & c_{22} & 0 \\ c_{31} & 0 & c_{33} \end{bmatrix}$$

obtained imposing four homogeneous constraints: $c_{12}=c_{21}=c_{23}=c_{32}=0$ so we can construct an R_c matrix of the following form:

$$R_c=\begin{bmatrix} 010000000 \\ 000100000 \\ 000001000 \\ 000000010 \end{bmatrix}$$

Proceeding as usual we arrive at the system:

$$\begin{bmatrix} c_{22} & 0 & 0 \\ -c_{11} & 0 & c_{13} \\ -c_{31} & 0 & c_{33} \\ 0 & 0 & -c_{22} \end{bmatrix} \cdot \begin{bmatrix} x_1 \\ x_2 \\ x_3 \end{bmatrix} = [0]$$

The second column of the coefficient matrix is [0], so the system accepts every x_2 as a solution. The model is unidentified and the non-identification rank is 1 (i.e. the difference between the number of column and the actual rank of the 'identification matrix').

This example is connected to the Bernanke.src procedure (last version 1990) created by Thomas Doan for the RATS econometric package. In the introduction the author mentions the concept of weak identification with respect to an AB-model where constraints of the same form as the ones we have imposed hold, except for one parameter which, instead of being constrained to be zero, has a free estimate close to zero.

The difficulties associated with the model, outlined by Doan, are due to the fact that in these cases we are facing a structure near to be block diagonal and the parameter close to zero is the one which connects two different blocks, so the iterative algorithm can easily fail to achieve convergence.

Following the approach of this monograph, there seems to be no room for an ambiguous concept like weak identification of some parameters: the whole set of parameters are either identified or non-identified. In our view, the problem faced by Doan is one of numerical difficulties in estimation of a set of identified parameters.

AB-model

For the AB-model we follow the identification condition outlined in section 4, so our model is identified if the system:

$$\begin{cases} R_a\,(A\otimes BB')\,z=[0] \\ R_b\,(B'\otimes BB')\,(\tilde{D}_n\,x-z)=[0] \end{cases}$$

has the unique solution $x=[0]$ and $z=[0]$. In the example below, we will proceed by solving the first sub-system and then inserting the solutions in the second one.

EXAMPLE 5

We start defining the A and B matrices:

$$A=\begin{bmatrix} 1 & 0 & 0 \\ a_{21} & 1 & 0 \\ 0 & a_{32} & 1 \end{bmatrix},\ B=\begin{bmatrix} b_{11} & 0 & b_{13} \\ 0 & b_{22} & 0 \\ 0 & 0 & b_{33} \end{bmatrix}$$

obtained imposing the homogeneous constraints $a_{12}=a_{13}=a_{23}=a_{31}=0$, $b_{12}=b_{21}=b_{23}=b_{31}=b_{32}=0$ and the non-homogeneous constraints $a_{11}=a_{22}=a_{33}=1$.

We introduce this constraints in the system by means of the following R matrices:

$$R_a=\begin{bmatrix} 100000000 \\ 001000000 \\ 000100000 \\ 000010000 \\ 000000100 \\ 000000010 \\ 000000001 \end{bmatrix} \text{ and } R_b=\begin{bmatrix} 010000000 \\ 001000000 \\ 000100000 \\ 000001000 \\ 000000010 \end{bmatrix}$$

Now we can solve the first sub-system:

$$R_a\,(A \otimes BB')\, z = [0]$$

where

$$R_a(A \otimes BB') =$$

$$\begin{bmatrix} b_{11}^2+b_{13}^2 & 0 & b_{33}b_{13} & 0 & 0 & 0 & 0 & 0 & 0 \\ b_{33}b_{13} & 0 & b_{33}^2 & 0 & 0 & 0 & 0 & 0 & 0 \\ a_{21}(b_{11}^2+b_{13}^2) & 0 & a_{21}b_{33}b_{13} & b_{11}^2+b_{13}^2 & 0 & b_{33}b_{13} & 0 & 0 & 0 \\ 0 & a_{21}b_{22}^2 & 0 & 0 & b_{22}^2 & 0 & 0 & 0 & 0 \\ 0 & 0 & 0 & a_{32}(b_{11}^2+b_{13}^2) & 0 & a_{32}b_{33}b_{13} & b_{11}^2+b_{13}^2 & 0 & b_{33}b_{13} \\ 0 & 0 & 0 & 0 & a_{32}b_{22}^2 & 0 & 0 & b_{22}^2 & 0 \\ 0 & 0 & 0 & a_{32}b_{13}b_{33} & 0 & a_{32}b_{33}^2 & b_{33}b_{13} & 0 & b_{33}^2 \end{bmatrix}$$

Substituting $b_{11}^2+b_{13}^2 = c$ and $b_{33}\,b_{13} = d$, we have to solve

$$\begin{bmatrix} c & 0 & d & 0 & 0 & 0 & 0 & 0 & 0 \\ d & 0 & b_{33}^2 & 0 & 0 & 0 & 0 & 0 & 0 \\ a_{21}c & 0 & a_{21}d & c & 0 & d & 0 & 0 & 0 \\ 0 & a_{21}b_{22}^2 & 0 & 0 & b_{22}^2 & 0 & 0 & 0 & 0 \\ 0 & 0 & 0 & a_{32}c & 0 & a_{32}d & c & 0 & d \\ 0 & 0 & 0 & 0 & a_{32}b_{22}^2 & 0 & 0 & b_{22}^2 & 0 \\ 0 & 0 & 0 & a_{32}b_{13}b_{33} & 0 & a_{32}b_{33}^2 & d & 0 & b_{33}^2 \end{bmatrix} z = [0]$$

which has the ∞^2 solutions (z_8 and z_9 are parameters):

$$z_1 = 0$$

$$z_2 = \frac{1}{a_{32}a_{21}} z_8$$

$$z_3 = 0$$

$$z_4 = \frac{d}{c\, a_{32}} z_9$$

$$z_5 = -\frac{1}{a_{32}} z_8$$

$$z_6 = -\frac{1}{a_{32}} z_9$$

$$z_7 = -\frac{d}{c} z_8$$

$$z_8 = z_8$$

$$z_9 = z_9.$$

Now we can insert the z vector in the second sub-system:

$$R_b\,(B'\otimes BB')\,(\tilde{D}_n x - z) = [0]$$

where

$$R_b\,(B'\otimes BB') = \begin{bmatrix} 0 & b_{11}b_{22}^2 & 0 & 0 & 0 & 0 & 0 & 0 & 0 \\ b_{11}d & 0 & b_{11}b_{33}^2 & 0 & 0 & 0 & 0 & 0 & 0 \\ 0 & 0 & 0 & b_{22}c & 0 & b_{22}d & 0 & 0 & 0 \\ 0 & 0 & 0 & b_{22}d & 0 & b_{22}b_{33}^2 & 0 & 0 & 0 \\ 0 & b_{13}b_{22}^2 & 0 & 0 & 0 & 0 & 0 & b_{33}b_{22}^2 & 0 \end{bmatrix}$$

and

$$\tilde{D}_n x - z = \begin{bmatrix} -z_1 \\ x_1 - z_2 \\ x_2 - z_3 \\ -x_1 - z_4 \\ -z_5 \\ x_3 - z_6 \\ -x_2 - z_7 \\ -x_3 - z_8 \\ -z_9 \end{bmatrix}$$

so we have to solve the system:

$$b_{11}\, b_{22}^2\,(x_1 - z_2) = 0 \qquad (1)$$

$$-z_1 b_{11} d + b_{11} b_{33}^2\,(x_2 - z_3) = 0 \qquad (2)$$

$$b_{22}c(-x_1 - z_4) + b_{22}d(x_3 - z_6) = 0 \qquad (3)$$

$$b_{22}d(-x_1 - z_4) + b_{22}b_{33}^2(x_3 - z_6) = 0 \qquad (4)$$

$$b_{13}b_{22}^2(x_1 - z_2) + b_{33}b_{22}^2(-x_3 - z_8) = 0. \qquad (5)$$

Substituting to $z_1 \ldots z_7$ their values with respect to z_8 and z_9, obtained from the first sub-system, we get:

$$x_1 = \frac{1}{a_{32}a_{21}} z_8 \tag{1'}$$

$$x_2 = 0 \tag{2'}$$

$$-cx_1 + dx_3 = 0 \tag{3'}$$

$$-dx_1 + \left(\frac{b_{33}^2}{a_{32}} - \frac{d^2}{ca_{32}} \right) z_9 + b_{33}^2 x_3 = 0 \tag{4'}$$

$$x_3 = -z_8. \tag{5'}$$

Now let us focus our attention on equation (3') where:

$$\left(d - \frac{c}{a_{32}a_{21}} \right) z_8 = 0 \Rightarrow z_8 = 0 \tag{3''}$$

which yields: $x_1 = 0$ and $x_3 = 0$ in (1') and (4') respectively.

Now looking at equation (4'), after some substitutions, we remain with:

$$\left(\frac{b_{33}}{a_{32}} - \frac{b_{13}}{a_{32}a_{21}} \right) z_9 = 0 \Rightarrow z_9 = 0 \tag{4''}$$

Inserting $z_8 = z_9 = 0$ in the first sub-system we get $z_1 \ldots z_7 = 0$, so the system is identified. In the same way we can get a generally over-identified model, simply adding - for example - the homogeneous constraint $a_{32} = 0$ so the A matrix becomes:

$$A = \begin{bmatrix} 1 & 0 & 0 \\ a_{21} & 1 & 0 \\ 0 & 0 & 1 \end{bmatrix}$$

and a possible form for R_a is:

$$R_a = \begin{bmatrix} 1&0&0&0&0&0&0&0&0 \\ 0&0&1&0&0&0&0&0&0 \\ 0&0&0&1&0&0&0&0&0 \\ 0&0&0&0&1&0&0&0&0 \\ 0&0&0&0&0&1&0&0&0 \\ 0&0&0&0&0&0&1&0&0 \\ 0&0&0&0&0&0&0&1&0 \\ 0&0&0&0&0&0&0&0&1 \end{bmatrix}$$

Calculations for this example will not be included since they are very similar to those developed earlier.

APPENDIX D

by Antonio Lanzarotti and Mario Seghelini

Introduction

In order to allow a practical use of the instruments provided in the previous pages, we have developed two procedures working as additional instructions of the RATS econometric package (for further details see Doan (1990) chapter 4).

The first procedure, called SVAR.SRC listed below, performs identification analysis and FIML estimation of all the three models. It considers the K and C models as particular cases of the AB model. This approach forced us to tackle the identification problem using sets of formulae that are different though equivalent to those already introduced in this monograph. Though old formulae were more easily treatable and symbolically more meaningful, the new ones require that constraints are expressed only in explicit form.

We suggest that the problem can be better understood starting from the V matrix defined in section 4 as follows

$$V\left[\frac{vecA}{vecB}\right]=\left[\begin{array}{c} 2\left[\begin{array}{c|c} K^{-1}\otimes B'^{-1} & [0] \\ \hline [0] & -(I\otimes B'^{-1}) \end{array}\right]\left[\begin{array}{c|c} N_n & N_n \\ \hline N_n & N_n \end{array}\right]\left[\begin{array}{c|c} K'^{-1}\otimes B^{-1} & [0] \\ \hline [0] & -(I\otimes B^{-1}) \end{array}\right] \\ \hline \begin{array}{c|c} R_a & [0] \\ \hline [0] & R_b \end{array} \end{array}\right]$$

premultiplying by the block diagonal matrix

$$\frac{1}{2}\left[\begin{array}{c|c|c|c} K\otimes B' & [0] & [0] & [0] \\ \hline [0] & -[I\otimes B'] & [0] & [0] \\ \hline [0] & [0] & 2\,I_{r_a} & [0] \\ \hline [0] & [0] & [0] & 2\,I_{r_b} \end{array}\right]$$

we get

$$V^{*}\left[\frac{vecA}{vecB}\right]=2\left[\begin{array}{c}\left[\begin{array}{c|c}\frac{N_n}{N_n} & \frac{N_n}{N_n}\end{array}\right]\left[\begin{array}{c|c}\frac{K'^{-1}\otimes B^{-1}}{[0]} & \frac{[0]}{-(I\otimes B^{-1})}\end{array}\right]\\ \begin{array}{c|c}\frac{R_a}{[0]} & \frac{[0]}{R_b}\end{array}\end{array}\right]$$

of the same order and rank as V.

To state the necessary and sufficient identification conditions, we consider the system

$$V^{*}\left[\frac{vecA}{vecB}\right]y=[0]$$

which must have the unique solution $y=[0]$. Supposing that the $2n^2\times 1$ vector can be written as $y=\left[\frac{z}{w}\right]$, the system can be split into two parts.

We can therefore write two connected systems of equations:

$$\left[\begin{array}{c|c}\frac{N_n}{N_n} & \frac{N_n}{N_n}\end{array}\right]\left[\begin{array}{c|c}\frac{K'^{-1}\otimes B^{-1}}{[0]} & \frac{[0]}{-(I\otimes B^{-1})}\end{array}\right]\left[\frac{z}{w}\right]=[0] \tag{1}$$

$$\left[\begin{array}{c|c}\frac{R_a}{[0]} & \frac{[0]}{R_b}\end{array}\right]\left[\frac{z}{w}\right]=[0] \tag{2}$$

Solving sub-system (2), we obtain

$$\begin{cases} z=S_a\,\gamma_a \\ w=S_b\,\gamma_b \end{cases}$$

Inserting the two solutions into sub-system (1), we get:

$$V^{**}\left[\frac{\gamma_a}{\gamma_b}\right]=[0]$$

where

$$V^{**}=\left[\begin{array}{c|c}\frac{N_n}{N_n} & \frac{N_n}{N_n}\end{array}\right]\left[\begin{array}{c|c}\frac{K'^{-1}\otimes B^{-1}}{[0]} & \frac{[0]}{-(I\otimes B^{-1})}\end{array}\right]S \tag{3}$$

and

$$S=\left[\begin{array}{cc} S_a & [0] \\ [0] & S_b \end{array}\right]$$

Now we have to analyse the (column) rank of V^{**} which is a $2n^2 \times (l_a + l_b)$ matrix. The model is identified if this matrix has full column rank.

Simple calculations yield:

$$V^{**} = \left[\begin{array}{c|c} N_n (K'^{-1} \otimes B^{-1})\, S_a & -N_n (I \otimes B^{-1})\, S_b \\ \hline N_n (K'^{-1} \otimes B^{-1})\, S_a & -N_n (I \otimes B^{-1})\, S_b \end{array}\right].$$

We can obviously focus our attention either on its upper or lower part since they are equal.

We can finally confine our efforts to checking the rank of

$$\left[N_n (K'^{-1} \otimes B^{-1})\, S_a \;\middle|\; -N_n (I \otimes B^{-1})\, S_b \right].$$

or, substituting K'^{-1} with $B'A'^{-1}$, the rank of

$$\left[N_n (B'A'^{-1} \otimes B^{-1})\, S_a \;\middle|\; -N_n (I \otimes B^{-1})\, S_b \right]. \tag{4}$$

Now it is easy to note that the K model and the C model identification analysis are embedded in the previous formula as sub-cases.

In the K model analysis we simply have $A = K$, $B = I$ and $S = \begin{bmatrix} S_a \\ \hline [0] \end{bmatrix}$, so we have to study the rank of

$$\left[N_n (K'^{-1} \otimes I)\, S_a \right]$$

The same arguments hold for the C model identification analysis with $A = I$, $B = C$ and $S = \begin{bmatrix} [0] \\ \hline S_b \end{bmatrix}$,

getting

$$\left[-N_n (I \otimes B^{-1})\, S_b \right]$$

Notice that in matrix (4) the number of columns (equal to $l_a + l_b$) decreases the more the model is constrained. This makes numerical evaluation easier.

For the FIML estimator, the formulae of section 4 are used allowing for the presence of a step-length factor (λ) whose function is to reduce the width of the parameter movements between two iterations of the scoring algorithm.

$$\begin{bmatrix}\gamma_a\\ \gamma_b\end{bmatrix}_{n+1}=\begin{bmatrix}\gamma_a\\ \gamma_b\end{bmatrix}_n+\lambda\left(I_T\begin{bmatrix}\gamma_a\\ \gamma_b\end{bmatrix}_n\right)^{-1}\cdot f\begin{bmatrix}\gamma_a\\ \gamma_b\end{bmatrix}_n=\begin{bmatrix}\gamma_a\\ \gamma_b\end{bmatrix}_n+\lambda\, DIR_n$$

The λ factor, suggested by many authors (see, for example, Harvey 1990, p. 124),is defined here as:

$$\lambda=\frac{maxls}{length} \qquad \text{if } length>maxls$$

$$\lambda=1 \qquad \text{otherwise}$$

Where $length = \max |DIR_{n,i}|$

and *maxls* is the chosen maximum movement of parameters between two iterations.

The SVAR.SRC procedure

The RATS package compiles our procedure with command[1]

SOURCE SVAR.SRC

and runs it with

@SVAR(OPTIONS) SIGMA START SA SB DA DB

The input parameters are as follows:

SIGMA: The estimated variance covariance matrix of the first-stage VAR (stored by option OUTSIGMA=SIGMA under the ESTIMATE command).

START: The vector of $\tilde{\gamma}$ starting values for the scoring algorithm (as remarked earlier, this is the crux of the whole analysis).

SA: The matrix of the coefficients of the constraints in the *A* matrix. In order to build a C-model, one should DECLARE SA as a 1×1 matrix

---

1 Before running our SVAR procedures, basic memory allocation must be reset with the command BMA COMPILE=4000 LOCAL=60

and set SA = [0]. The procedure will then exclude the presence of free parameters in the *A* matrix.

SB: the same as SA with respect to the *B* matrix. In order to analyse the K-model, one should declare SB as a 1×1 matrix and set SB = [0].

DA: The vector representing the non-homogeneous part of the constraints imposed on the *A* matrix. Working with a C-model, DA should be set as equal to *vecI*.

DB: The same as DA with respect to the *B* matrix. For the K-model, DB should be set as equal to *vecI*.

Screen output gives the estimated *A* and *B* matrices (or *K*, *C*, etc.), the result of the over-identification test (if required) and a table containing what follows:

- estimated coefficients of *A* and *B*;
- the standard errors;
- t-test values and significance levels.

The following options are also available (default values are included in square brackets):

REC: maximum number of iterations [100]

TEST: over-identification LR test [test]/notest

MAXLS: maximum movement between iterations [1]

The procedure leaves the following matrices and vectors as accessible variables:

A, B: the matrices of the estimated coefficients

ABSIGMA: the estimated variance covariance matrix of the $vec(A \mid B)$ vector

TSTAT: the vector containing the t-statistic of *A* and *B* coefficients

GAMMA: the estimated $\tilde{\gamma}$ vector.

SVAR.SRC listing

The procedure is listed below[2]

```
*****************************************************************************
*                        ***********************                            *
*                        *  PROCEDURE SVAR.SRC  *                           *
*                        ***********************                            *
*              by Antonio Lanzarotti and Mario Seghelini                    *
*                        University of Pavia                                *
*                                                                           *
*  THIS PROCEDURE IMPOSES,TROUGH A SET OF CONSTRAINTS,A 'STRUCTURAL' FORM   *
*  ON A VAR MODEL, CHECKS FOR IDENTIFICATION CONDITIONS AND PERFORMS A      *
*  FIML ESTIMATION OF THE 'STRUCTURAL' PARAMETERS.                          *
*                                                                           *
*  BMA requirement:  Compile 4000 Local 60                                  *
*  Syntax:           @svar(options) sigma start sa sb da db                 *
*                    sigma= estimated V-Cov of VAR residuals                *
*                    start= vector of starting values for gamma             *
*                    sa= matrix of the explicit form constraints on A       *
*                    sb= matrix of the explicit form constraints on B       *
*                    da= vector of the non-homogeneous part of              *
*                        constraints on A                                   *
*                    db= vector of the non-homogeneous part of              *
*                        constraints on B                                   *
*  Options:          rec= maximum number of iterations [100]                *
*                    [test]/notest= over-identification LR test             *
*                    maxls= maximum movement of the parameters between      *
*                           two iterations of the scoring algorithm.        *
*                                                                           *
* NOTE: If you want to build up a K (or C) model, all you need is to declare *
* sb (sa) as a 1x1 matrix, set it equal to [0] and input db=vec(I) (or      *
* da=vec(I)).                                                               *
*                                                                           *
****************** PLEASE  WAIT  WHILE  COMPILING ***************************
output noecho
procedure svar sigma start sa sb da db
*
option rec integer 100
option test switch 1
option maxls real 1.0
*
type symm sigma
type rect sa sb
type vect da db start
```

---

2 We have run our procedures on an Apple Macintosh® SE 30 with the following configuration: Motorola 68030 CPU at 16 MHz, 68882 math coprocessor, 8 Mb RAM memory.

```
      ******
      ******   This section declares the variables.
      ******
declare rect a b
declare symm absigma
declare vect tstat gamma
local int l l1 l2 rni nsq i j iters degrees
local rect s tenx h v v1 v2 idmat k ktmu derk derk1 derk2
local symm infk infgamma rsigma mid mid2 ms
local vect d vecab auto veck vecktmu z fveck fgamma dir signlev
local real cvcri lenght lambda det1 det2 lrtest signif zeta
local label name name1 name2
*
inquire(matrix=sigma) n
inquire(matrix=sa) ansq afree
if ansq==1
  ieval afree=0
inquire(matrix=sb) bnsq bfree
if bnsq==1
  ieval bfree=0
ieval nsq=n**2
ieval l=afree+bfree
*
dim s(2*nsq,l) tenx(nsq,nsq) h(n,n) v(nsq,2*nsq) v1(nsq,nsq) v2(nsq,nsq)
dim a(n,n) b(n,n) idmat(nsq,l) mid(n,n) mid2(nsq,nsq) ms(l,l)
dim d(2*nsq) gamma(l) vecab(2*nsq) auto(l)
      ******
      ******   This section defines the S matrix  and the d vector
      ******   (Sargan 1988, p.33) according to the selected model.
      ******
if afree==0
  {
  do i=1,nsq
    do j=1,bfree
     eval s(i,j)=0.0
     eval s(i+nsq,j)=sb(i,j)
    end do j
  end do i
  eval name='C'
  }
else if bfree==0
  {
  do i=1,nsq
    do j=1,afree
      eval s(i,j)=sa(i,j)
      eval s(i+nsq,j)=0.0
    end do j
  end do i
  eval name='K'
  }
else
  {
  do i=1,nsq
    do j=1,afree
      eval s(i,j)=sa(i,j)
      eval s(i+nsq,j)=0.0
    end do j
```

```
    do j=afree+1,l
      eval s(i,j)=0.0
      eval s(i+nsq,j)=sb(i,j-afree)
    end do j
  end do i
  eval name='AB'
  }
do i=1,nsq
  eval d(i)=da(i)
  eval d(i+nsq)=db(i)
end do i
      ******
      ******  This section defines the commutation matrix (tenx)
      ******  following Magnus (1988, p.37).
      ******
matrix tenx=const(0.0)
do l1=1,n
  do l2=1,n
    ewise h(i,j)=(i==l1.and.j==l2)
    matrix tenx=tenx+kroneker(h,tr(h))
  end do l2
end do l1
      ******
      ******  This section checks numerically the identification conditions.
      ******
matrix gamma=ran(1.0)
overlay vecab(1) with a(n,n)
overlay vecab(nsq+1) with b(n,n)
matrix vecab=s*gamma+d
*
overlay v(1,1) with v1(nsq,nsq)
overlay v(1, nsq+1) with v2(nsq,nsq)
matrix mid2=iden(1.0)
matrix mid=iden(1.0)
mat v1=(mid2+tenx)*(kroneker(tr(inv(a)*b),inv(b)))
mat v2=scale(-1.0)*(mid2+tenx)*(kroneker(mid,inv(b)))
mat idmat=v*s
mat ms=tr(idmat)*idmat
*
eigen ms auto
ieval rni=0
do i=1,l
  if auto(i)<.1e-10
    ieval rni=rni+1
end do i
display 'ms eigenvalues vector'
display ' '
write auto
if rni==0
  if l==n*(n+1)/2
    display 'The ' name '-model is just-identified.'
  else
    display 'The ' name '-model  is over-identified.'
else
  {
  display 'The ' name '-model is unidentified.'
  display ' '
```

```
  display 'The non-identification rank is ' rni
  return
  }
      ******
      ******   This section performs a FIML estimation of the structural
      ******   parameters by means of the scoring algorithm (see, for example
      ******   Harvey 1990, p.134)
      ******
dim k(n,n) ktmu(n,n) derk(nsq,2*nsq) derk1(nsq,nsq) derk2(nsq,nsq)
dim infk(nsq,nsq) infgamma(1,1) rsigma(n,n) veck(nsq) vecktmu(nsq)
dim z(1) fveck(nsq) fgamma(1) dir(1) tstat(2*nsq) signlev(2*nsq)
dim absigma(2*nsq,2*nsq)
*
overlay veck(1) with k(n,n)
overlay vecktmu(1) with ktmu(n,n)
overlay derk(1,1) with derk1(nsq,nsq)
overlay derk(1,nsq+1) with derk2(nsq,nsq)
*
ieval iters=0
mat gamma=start
*
until cvcri<.1e-6
  {
  mat z=gamma
  mat vecab=s*gamma+d
  mat k=inv(b)*a
  mat ktmu=tr(inv(k))
  mat derk1=kroneker(mid,inv(b))
  mat derk2=scale(-1.0)*kroneker(tr(k),inv(b))
  mat infk=kroneker(inv(k),mid)*(mid2+tenx)*kroneker(ktmu,mid)*scale(nobs)
  mat infgamma=tr(s)*tr(derk)*infk*derk*s
  mat fveck=scale(nobs)*(vecktmu-kroneker(sigma,mid)*veck)
  mat fgamma=tr(s)*tr(derk)*fveck
  mat dir=inv(infgamma)*fgamma
  write dir
  mat zeta = tr(fgamma)*fgamma
  display zeta
  mat lenght=maxvalue(abs(dir))
  if lenght>maxls
    eval lambda=maxls/lenght
  else
    eval lambda=1.0
  mat gamma=gamma+scale(lambda)*dir
  ieval iters=iters+1
  display iters
  display ' '
  write gamma
  mat z=z-gamma
  mat cvcri=maxvalue(abs(z))
  if iters==rec
    break
  }
if cvcri<.1e-6
  display 'Convergence achieved after' iters 'iterations'
else
  {
  display 'Convergence not achieved after' rec 'iterations'
```

```
   display 'Convergence value:' cvcri
   }
mat vecab=s*gamma+d
if name=='K'
   {
   display 'Estimated K matrix'
   write a
   }
else if name=='C'
   {
   display 'Estimated C matrix'
   write b
   }
else
   {
   display 'Estimated A matrix'
   write a
   display ' '
   display 'Estimated B matrix'
   write b
   }
*
mat absigma=s*inv(infgamma)*tr(s)
      ******
      ******   This section provides a LR over-identification test.
      ******
if test
   {
   ieval degrees=(n+1)*n/2-1
   if degrees==0
     display 'The' name 'model is just identified. No test is possible.'
   else
     {
     mat rsigma=inv(a)*b*tr(b)*tr(inv(a))
     mat det1=log(det(sigma))
     mat det2=log(det(rsigma))+trace(inv(rsigma)*sigma)
     eval lrtest=(det2-det1-n)*nobs
     cdf(noprint) chisqr lrtest degrees
     fetch signif=signif
     display 'OVER-IDENTIFICATION LR TEST '
     display ' '
     display 'Chi-squared(' degrees ')=' lrtest '  Signficance level=' signif
     display ' '
     }
   }
      ******
      ******   This section computes the values and the significance levels
      ******   of the t-statistics of the structural parameters.
      ******
do i=1,2*nsq
  if absigma(i,i)<>0.0
    {
    eval tstat(i)=vecab(i)/sqrt(absigma(i,i))
    cdf(noprint) ttest tstat(i) (nobs-1)
    fetch signif=signif
    eval signlev(i)=signif
    }
```

```
   else
     {
     eval tstat(i)=0.0
     eval signlev(i)=0.0
     }
end do i
dis '  STATISTICS ON' name '-MODEL PARAMETERS '
dis ' ************************************************************************** '
dis ' |  Parameter |  Coefficent |  Std.Error  |   T-value   | Sign. Level | '
dis ' ************************************************************************** '
if name=='AB'
   {
   eval name1='A'
   eval name2='B'
   }
else
   {
   eval name1='K'
   eval name2='C'
   }
if name=='K'.or.name=='AB'
   {
   do i=1,n
     do j=1,n
       dis @1 '|' @3 name1  @5 '(' @6 ## i @8 ',' @9 ## j @11 ')' $
           @14 '|' @15 a(i,j) @28 '|' $
           @29 sqrt(absigma((j-1)*n+i,(j-1)*n+i)) $
           @42 '|' @43 tstat((j-1)*n+i) @56 '|' @57 signlev((j-1)*n+i) @70 '|'
     end do j
   end do i
   }
if name=='C'.or.name=='AB'
   {
   do i=1,n
     do j=1,n
       dis @1 '|' @3 name2 @5 '(' @6 ## i @8 ',' @9 ## j @11 ')' $
        @14 '|' @15 b(i,j) @28 '|' $
        @29 sqrt(absigma((j-1)*n+i+nsq,(j-1)*n+i+nsq)) $
        @42 '|' @43 tstat((j-1)*n+i+nsq) @56 '|' @57 signlev((j-1)*n+i+nsq) $
        @70 '|'
     end do j
   end do i
   }
dis ' **************************************************************************'
display
display 'Now you can access to the following matrices and vectors:'
display 'a, b      containing the structural parameters'
display 'absigma   containing the estimated v-cov of vec[a|b]'
display 'tstat     containing the t-statistics of the structural parameters'
display 'gamma     containing the estimated free elements of vec[a|b]'
end
```

The VMA.SRC procedure

In addition to the procedure listed above, we propose one further procedure, called VMA.SRC, which performs the estimation of the Structured Impulse Response Functions and Forecast Error Variance Decomposition with asymptotic confidence bounds evaluated following section 5 and taking as input part of the result of the SVAR.SRC procedure. A recent paper by Griffiths and Lütkepohl (1990) indicates that confidence intervals for impulse response functions, based on asymptotic theory behave in a better way with respect to normal simulation and bootstrapping intervals, under different sampling and distributional assumptions.

The RATS package compiles[3] the procedure with the instruction:

SOURCE VMA.SRC

and runs it with

@VMA(OPTIONS) A B ABSIGMA IXIX VARPARAM

The respective input paramaters are as follows:

A,B: the matrices of the estimated structural parameters of the SVAR model;

ABSIGMA: the estimated variance covariance matrix of $vec[A \mid B]$;

IXIX: the $(X'X)^{-1}$matrix introduced earlier. It can be obtained with the instruction KFSET IXIX included within the commands needed to set up a VAR model (we are using here the same notation as Doan (1990) for the $(X'X)^{-1}$ matrix, ie, a transposed notation with respect to the one used in this monograph).

VARPARAM: the $(n \times np)$ matrix containing the estimated coefficients of the first-stage VAR; its form is as follows:

$$\text{VARPARAM} = \left[A_1 \mid A_2 \mid \ldots \mid A_p\right]$$

---

3 Basic memory allocation is: BMA COMPILE 4000 LOCAL 60.

This matrix can be built by saving the VAR coefficients in n series and then storing them by the following instructions

```
DO serie = 1,n
  DO i = 1,n
    DO j = 1,p
      EVAL VARPARAM(serie, (j-1)n + i) = serie((i-1)p+j)
    END DO j
  END DO i
END DO serie
```

where n = number of variables and p = order of the VAR.

Notice that the VARPARAM does not have to contain the coefficients of the deterministic components of the VAR model.

The following options are also available:

ERROR = Forecast Error Variance Decomposition parameters

S1 = order of the VMA representation [20]

S2 = number of steps for FEVD (obviously S2≤S1) [15].

CLEVEL = confidence level for the asymptotic bounds [0.05].

The VMA's output gives the following matrices as accessible variables:

IRF = contains the non-structured VMA parameters

IMPULSE = structured parameters

IRFVAR = contains the variances of the IMPULSE parameters.

IRFBOUND = widths of the structured parameters asymptotic confidence bounds.

Choosing ERROR option one can get:

FEVD = containing the Forecast Error Variance Decomposition parameteres

DECVAR = containing the FEVD parameters variances

DECBOUND = containing FEVD parameters asymptotic bounds[4]

---

4 The matrices in output have all the same structure. For example, IRF contains in its s-th column the vec form of the matrix on the non-structured impulse response functions after (s-1) steps; FEVD contains in its s-th column the vec form of the matrix of s-steps forecast error, and so on.

VMA.SRC listing

The procedure is listed below.

```
*****************************************************************************
*                          **********************                           *
*                          * PROCEDURE VMA.SRC  *                           *
*                          **********************                           *
*               by Antonio Lanzarotti and Mario Seghelini                   *
*                          University of Pavia                              *
*                                                                           *
*  THIS PROCEDURE RETURNS THE VMA REPRESENTATION OF A STRUCTURAL VAR MODEL  *
*  AND COMPUTES BY ASYMPTOTIC FORMULAE THE BOUNDS AROUND THE IMPULSES AT A  *
*  PRESELECTED CONFIDENCE LEVEL.FORECAST ERROR VARIANCE DECOMPOSITION (WITH *
*  ASYMPTOTIC BOUNDS) IS ALSO PROVIDED, AS AN OPTION.                       *
*                                                                           *
*  BMA requirement:   Compile 4000  Local 60                                *
*  Syntax:            @vma(options) a b absigma ixix varparam               *
*                     a, b = matrices of structural parameters              *
*                     absigma = estimated V-Cov matrix of vec[a|b]          *
*                     ixix = inv(x'x)                                       *
*                     varparam = matrix of the first stage VAR parameters   *
*  Options:           s1 = order of the VMA representation [20]             *
*                     error = forecast error variance decomposition  [1]    *
*                     s2 = order for the FEVD [15]                          *
*                     clevel = bounds confidence level [0.05]               *
*                                                                           *
*                                                                           *
********************** PLEASE WAIT WHILE COMPILING **************************
output noecho
procedure vma a b absigma ixix varparam
*
type symm absigma ixix
type rect a b varparam
*
option s1 integer 20
option s2 integer 15
option clevel real .05
option error switch 1
      ******
      ******   This section declares the variables
      ******
local rect apower k derk derk1 derk2 amat g jota xjota ggg gi gj sigmahh
local rect wold swold woldi woldj mh wh p2 zh uu dz f uuu iu sss sigmah org
local symm sigma0 mid midnp sigmak sigmap fh pp pd
local symm  sigmawh mid2
local vector normal vecsw u veci
local integer i j n nsq s e np x y npar h step1 step2 p
local real z asum bsum
*
declare rect irfvar irfbound impulse irf
declare rect fevd decvar decbound tenx
*
inquire(matrix=ixix) npar
```

```
inquire(matrix=a) n n
inquire(matrix=varparam) n np
ieval nsq=n**2
ieval step1=s1
ieval step2=s2
if step1.lt.step2
  {
   disp '**** WARNING ****'
   disp 'FEVD order exceed the VMA representation order.This has no meaning.'
   disp 'The procedure will set s2=s1'
   ieval step2=step1
  }
*
dim apower(np,np) k(n,n) derk(nsq,nsq*2) derk1(nsq,nsq) derk2(nsq,nsq)
dim amat(np,np) g(nsq,n*np) jota(n,np) xjota(npar,np) wold(n,n) swold(n,n)
dim sigma0(nsq,nsq) mid(n,n) midnp(np,np) sigmak(nsq,nsq) sigmah(nsq,nsq)
dim sigmap(n*np,n*np) normal(20) irf(nsq,step1) org(npar,npar)
dim irfvar(nsq,step1) irfbound(nsq,step1) impulse(nsq,step1)
dim ggg(nsq*step1,n*np) gi(nsq,n*np) gj(nsq,n*np) sigmahh(nsq,nsq)
dim uu(nsq,nsq) dz(nsq,nsq) woldi(n,n) woldj(n,n) mh(n,n) fh(n,n) wh(n,n)
dim p2(n,n) zh(nsq,nsq*step2) sss(nsq*step2,nsq*step2)
dim pp(n,n) pd(n,n) tenx(nsq,nsq) sigmawh(nsq,nsq) mid2(nsq,nsq)
dim vecsw(nsq) veci(nsq) u(nsq) f(n,n) uuu(nsq,nsq) iu(nsq,nsq)
dim fevd(nsq,step2) decvar(nsq,step2) decbound(nsq,step2)
*
overlay derk(1,1) with derk1(nsq,nsq)
overlay derk(1,nsq+1) with derk2(nsq,nsq)
mat veci=const(0.0)
mat sss=const(0.0)
mat irfvar=const(0.0)
      ******
      ******   This section trasforms the IXIX matrix according to the
      ******   ordering adopted for the VARPARAM matrix.
      ******
ieval p=np/n
mat org=const(0.0)
do i=1,n
  do j=1,p
    eval org((j-1)*n+i,(i-1)*p+j)=1.0
  end do j
end do i
do i=np+1,npar
  eval org(i,i)=1.0
end do i
mat ixix=inv(tr(org))*ixix*inv(org)*scale(nobs)
*
do x=1,n
  eval veci(n*(x-1)+x)=1.0
end do x
      ******
      ******   This section computes the Sigma(0) matrix
      ******
matrix tenx=const(0.0)
do x=1,n
  do y=1,n
    ewise f(i,j)=(i==x.and.j==y)
    matrix tenx=tenx+kroneker(f,tr(f))
```

```
    end do y
  end do x
  mat absigma=absigma*scale(nobs)
  mat u=const(1.0)
  mat mid2=iden(1.0)
  mat mid=iden(1.0)
  mat midnp=iden(1.0)
  mat k=inv(b)*a
  mat asum=sum(a)
  mat bsum=sum(b)
  if asum==n
    ewise sigma0(i,j)=absigma(nsq+i,nsq+j)
  else
    {
    if bsum==n
      ewise sigmak(i,j)=absigma(i,j)
    else
      {
      mat derk1=kroneker(mid,inv(b))
      mat derk2=kroneker(tr(k),inv(b))*scale(-1.0)
      mat sigmak=derk*absigma*tr(derk)
      }
    mat sigma0=kroneker(tr(inv(k)),inv(k))*sigmak*kroneker(inv(k),tr(inv(k)))
    }
        ******
        ******   This section builds up the A matrix (here named AMAT) following
        ******   Lutkepohl (1989), p.372.
        ******
  mat amat=const(0.0)
  do i=1,n
    do j=1,np
      eval amat(i,j)=varparam(i,j)
    end do j
  end do i
  do i=1,np-n
    eval amat(n+i,i)=1.0
  end do i
  *
  mat jota=const(0.0)
  do i=1,n
    eval jota(i,i)=1.0
  end do i
        ******
        ******   This section returns the impulse response functions of the
        ******   structural VAR model.
        ******
  mat apower=midnp
  do e=1,step1
    mat wold=jota*apower*tr(jota)
    mat swold=wold*inv(k)
    do i=1,n
      do j=1,n
        eval irf((j-1)*n+i,e)=wold(i,j)
        eval impulse((j-1)*n+i,e)=swold(i,j)
      end do j
    end do i
    mat apower=apower*amat
```

```
end do e
      ******
      ******   This section performs the estimation of the Sigma(p) matrix
      ******   equivalent to the Sigma(alfa) matrix in Lutkepohl (1989),
      ******   p.374
      ******
mat xjota=const(0.0)
do i=1,np
  eval xjota(i,i)=1.0
end do i
mat sigmap=kroneker(tr(xjota)*ixix*xjota,inv(tr(k)*k))
      ******
      ******   This section computes the asyptotic confidence bounds on the
      ******   basis of the formulae of Lutkepohl (1989), p.373
      ******
display 'IRF STEP' 1
*
mat ggg=const(0.0)
do i=1,step1-1
  mat apower=midnp
  mat g=const(0.0)
  do s=1,i-1
    ewise wold(x,y)=irf((y-1)*n+x,i-s)
    mat g=g+kroneker(tr(inv(k))*jota*apower,wold)
    mat apower=apower*tr(amat)
  end do s
  do x=1,nsq
    do y=1,n*np
      eval ggg(x+nsq*i,y)=g(x,y)
    end do y
  end do x
end do i
*
do i=1,step1-1
  mat sigmah=const(0.0)
  ewise wold(x,y)=irf((y-1)*n+x,i+1)
  ewise g(x,y)=ggg(x+nsq*i,y)
  mat sigmah=g*sigmap*tr(g)+kroneker(mid,wold)*sigma0*tr(kroneker(mid,wold))
  do x=1,nsq
    eval irfvar(x,i+1)=sigmah(x,x)/nobs
    if error.and.i.lt.step2
    {
    do y=1,nsq
      eval sss(i*nsq+x,i*nsq+y)=sigmah(x,y)
    end do y
    }
  end do x
  display 'IRF STEP' i+1
end do i
*
do x=1,nsq
  eval irfvar(x,1)=sigma0(x,x)/nobs
  do y=1,nsq
    eval sss(x,y)=sigma0(x,y)
  end do y
end do x
      ******
```

```
      ******   This section computes the width of the asymptotic bounds
      ******   according to the selected significance level.
      ******
read(unit=input) normal
 2.57 2.33 2.17 2.01 1.96 1.88 1.81 1.75 1.69 1.64
 1.60 1.55 1.51 1.47 1.44 1.40 1.37 1.34 1.31 1.28
ieval e=fix(clevel*100+.5)
eval z=normal(e)
ewise irfbound(i,j)=z*sqrt(irfvar(i,j))
      ******
      ******   This section computes the forecast error variance decomposition
      ******   for the structural model (if required) and provides asymptotic
      ******   confidence bounds.
      ******
if error
  {
  display '**** WARNING ****'
  display 'The program is calculating the whole variance-covariance matrix of'
  display 'the VMA representation. For example this will take up to one hour'
  display 'for 15 steps in a five-variables system. PLEASE WAIT.'
  do i=0,step2-2
    do j=i+1,step2-1
display i j
     ewise gi(x,y)=ggg(x+nsq*i,y)
     ewise gj(x,y)=ggg(x+nsq*j,y)
     ewise woldi(x,y)=irf((y-1)*n+x,i+1)
     ewise woldj(x,y)=irf((y-1)*n+x,j+1)
     mat sigmahh=gi*sigmap*tr(gj)+kroneker(mid,woldi)*sigma0*    $
                   tr(kroneker(mid,woldj))
     do x=1,nsq
       do y=1,nsq
         eval sss(i*nsq+x,j*nsq+y)=sigmahh(x,y)
         eval sss(j*nsq+y,i*nsq+x)=sigmahh(x,y)
       end do y
     end do x
    end do j
  end do i
*
  mat fh=const(0.0)
  mat mh=const(0.0)
  mat wh=const(0.0)
  do h=0,step2-1
    ewise swold(x,y)=impulse((y-1)*n+x,h+1)
    ewise p2(x,y)=swold(x,y)**2
    mat mh=mh+p2
    mat pp=swold*tr(swold)
    ewise pd(x,y)=pp(x,y)*mid(x,y)
    mat fh=fh+pd
    mat wh=inv(fh)*mh
    do x=1,n
      do y=1,n
        eval fevd((y-1)*n+x,h+1)=wh(x,y)
      end do y
    end do x
    mat sigmawh=const(0.0)
    mat zh=const(0.0)
    do j=0,h
```

```
      ewise swold(x,y)=impulse((y-1)*n+x,j+1)
      ewise vecsw(x)=impulse(x,j+1)
      mat uu=u*tr(vecsw)
      ewise uu(x,y)=uu(x,y)*mid2(x,y)
      mat uuu=veci*tr(u)
      ewise iu(x,y)=uuu(x,y)*mid2(x,y)
      mat dz=scale(2.0)*kroneker(mid,inv(fh))*uu-kroneker(tr(wh),inv(fh))* $
              iu*(mid2+tenx)*kroneker(swold,mid)
      do x=1,nsq
        do y=1,nsq
          eval zh(x,j*nsq+y)=dz(x,y)
        end do y
      end do x
    end do j
    mat sigmawh=zh*sss*tr(zh)
    do x=1,nsq
      eval decvar(x,h+1)=sigmawh(x,x)/nobs
      eval decbound(x,h+1)=sqrt(sigmawh(x,x)/nobs)*z
    end do x
    display 'FEVD STEP' h+1
  end do h
  }
display 'Now you can access the following output matrices'
display 'IRFVAR     containing the structured VMA parameters variances'
display 'IMPULSE    containing the structured VMA parameters'
display 'IRF        containing the non-structured VMA parameters'
display 'IRFBOUND   the width of the confidence bounds'
if error
 {
  disp 'FEVD        containing fevd parameters'
  disp 'DECVAR      the parameters variances'
  disp 'DECBOUND    the width of fevd confidence bounds'
  }
end vma
```

References

BAILLIE, R.T. (1987), "Inference in Dynamic Models Containing 'Surprise' Variables", *Journal of Econometrics*, 35, 101-117.

BEKKER, P.A., D.S.G. POLLOCK (1986), "Identification of Linear Stochastic Models with Covariance Restrictions", *Journal of Econometrics*, 31, 179-208

BERNANKE, B. (1986), "Alternative Explanations of the Money-Income Correlation.", *Carnegie Rochester Conference Series on Public Policy*, 25, 49-99

BLANCHARD, O.J. (1986), "Empirical Structural Evidence on Wages, Prices and Employment in the U.S.", *NBER Working Paper n.*2044.

BLANCHARD, O.J. (1989), "A Traditional Interpretation of Macroeconomic Fluctuations.", *American Economic Review*, 79, 1146-1164.

BLANCHARD, O.J., D. QUAH (1989), "The Dynamic Effects of Aggregate Demand and Supply Disturbances", *American Economic Review*, 79, 655-673.

BLANCHARD, O.J., M.W.WATSON (1986), "Are Business Cycles All Alike?", in (edited by) R.Gordon, *The American Business Cycle: Continuity and Change*, NBER & University of Chicago Press, 123-156.

DHRYMES, P.J. (1978), *Mathematics for Econometrics*, Springer Verlag, New York.

DOAN, T.A. (1990), *RATS User's Manual, version 3.11*, VAR Econometrics.

ENGLE, R.F., C.V.J. GRANGER (1987), "Co-integration and Error Correction : Representation, Estimation and Testing" *Econometrica* , 55, 251-276.

GRIFFITHS, W., H. LÜTKEPOHL (1990), "Confidence Intervals for Impulse Responses from VAR Models: A Comparison of Asymptotic Theory and Simulation Approaches", *Arbeiten aus dem Institute für Statistik und Ökonometrik der Universität Kiel*, Working paper.

HARVEY, A.C. (1990), *The Econometric Analysis of Time Series*, LSE Handbook in Economics, Philip Allan.

HURCWIZ, L. (1962), "On the Structural Form of Interdependent Systems", in E. NAGEL, P. SUPPES, A. TARSKY (eds.), *Logic, Methodology and Philosophy of Science, Proceedings of the 1960 International Congress, Stanford University Press.*

HYLLEBERG, S., G.E. MIZON (1989), "Cointegration and Error Correction Mechanisms", *Economic Journal*, 99, 113-125.

JOHANSEN, S. (1988)," Statistical Analysis of Cointegrated Vectors" *Journal of Economics Dynamics and Control* , 12, 231-254.

JOHANSEN, S. (1989a), "Estimation and Hypothesis Testing of Cointegration Vectors in Gaussian Vector Autoregressive Models" *Institute of Mathematical Statistics, University of Copenhagen*, Working Paper.

JOHANSEN, S. (1989b), "Likelihood Based Inference on Cointegration .Theory and Applications", *Lecture Notes* prepared for a course on cointegration for C.I.D.E. Summer School, Libreria Editrice Cafoscarina.

KEATING, J.W. (1990), "Identifying VAR Models Under Rational Expectations", *Journal of Monetary Economics*, 25, 453-476.

LÜTKEPOHL, H. (1989), "A Note on the Asymptotic Distribution of Impulse Response Functions of Estimated VAR Models with Orthogonal Residuals", *Journal of Econometrics*, 42, 371-376.

LÜTKEPOHL, H. (1990), "Asymptotic Distribution of Impulse Response Functions and Forecast Error Variance Decompositions of Vector Autoregressive Models", *The Review of Economics and Statistics*, 72, 116-125

LÜTKEPOHL, H. (1991), *Introduction to Multiple Time Series Analysis*, Springer Verlag, New York.

LÜTKEPOHL, H., H.E. REIMERS (1990), "Impulse Response Analysis of Co-integrated Systems with an Application to German Money Demand",

Arbeiten aus dem Institute für Statistik und Ökonometric der Universität Kiel, Working Paper.

MAGNUS, J.R. (1988), *Linear Structures*, Charles Griffin & Co., London.

MAGNUS, J.R. , H. NEUDECKER (1988), *Matrix Differential Calculus with Applications in Statistics and Econometrics* , John Wiley & Sons, New York.

NELSON, C., H. KANG (1981), "Spurious Periodicity in Inappropriately Detrended Time Series", *Econometrica*, 49, 741-751.

PAGAN, A. (1986), "Two Stage and Related Estimators and their Applications.", *Review of Economic Studies*, LIII, 517-538.

PARK, J.Y. , P.C.B. PHILLIPS (1987), "Statistical Inference in Regressions with Integrated Processes:Part 2", *Cowles Foundation Discussion Paper*, nº.819.

PHILLIPS, P.C.B. (1991), "Optimal Inference in Cointegrated Systems", *Econometrica*, 59, 283-306.

POLLAK, R.A., T.J. WALES (1991), "The Likelihood Dominance Criterion: a New Approach to Model Selection", *Journal of Econometrics*, 47, 227-242.

POLLOCK, D.S.G. (1979), *The Algebra of Econometrics* , John Wiley & Sons, New York.

ROTHENBERG, T.J. (1971), "Identification in Parametric Models", *Econometrica, 39*, 577-791.

ROTHENBERG, T.J. (1973), *Efficient Estimation with A Priori Information*, Yale University Press, New Haven.

ROTHENBERG, T.J., L.T. LEENDERS (1964), "Efficient Estimation of Simultaneous Equation Systems", *Econometrica*,32, 57-76.

RUNKLE, D.E. (1987), "Vector Autoregressions and Reality", *Journal of Business & Economic Statistics*, 5, 437-442.

SARGAN, D. (1988), *Lectures on Advanced Econometric Theory*, Basil Blackwell, Oxford.

SERFLING, R.F. (1980), *Approximation Theorems of Mathematical Statistics,* John Wiley & Sons, New York.

SHAPIRO, M., M.W. WATSON (1988), "Sources of Business Cycle Fluctuations", *NBER Macroeconomic Annual*; MIT Press, 3, 111-156.

SIMS, C.A. (1980), "Macroeconomics and Reality", *Econometrica,* 48, 1-48.

SIMS, C.A. (1986), "Are Forecasting Models Usable for Policy Analysis?", *Federal Reserve Bank of Minneapolis Quarterly Review,* Winter, 2-16.

SIMS, C.A. (1988), "Identifying Policy Effects", in (edited by) R.C. BRYANT et al. *Empirical Macroeconomics for Interdipendent Economics,* Brookings Institutions, 305-321.

SIMS, C.A. , J.H. STOCK, M.W. WATSON (1990), "Inference in Linear Time Series Models with some Unit Roots.", *Econometrica* ,58, 113-144.

TSAY, R.S., G.C. TIAO (1986), "Asymptotic Properties of Multivariate Nonstationary Processes with Applications to Autoregressions." , *Annals of Statistics* ,18, 220-250.

WEGGE, L. (1965), "Identifiability Criteria for a System of Equations as a Whole", *Australian Journal of Statistics,* 7, 67-77.

WHITE, H. (1982), "Maximum Likelihood Estimation of Misspecified Models", *Econometrica,* 50, 1-26.

WHITE, H. (1983), "Estimation, Inference and Specification Analysis", *Discussion Paper n.* 83-26, University of California, San Diego.

WHITE, H. (1984), *Asymptotic Theory for Econometricians,* Academic Press, London.

Lecture Notes in Economics and Mathematical Systems

For information about Vols. 1–210 please contact your bookseller or Springer-Verlag

Vol. 211: P. van den Heuvel, The Stability of a Macroeconomic System with Quantity Constraints. VII, 169 pages. 1983.

Vol. 212: R. Sato and T. Nôno, Invariance Principles and the Structure of Technology. V, 94 pages. 1983.

Vol. 213: Aspiration Levels in Bargaining and Economic Decision Making. Proceedings, 1982. Edited by R. Tietz. VIII, 406 pages. 1983.

Vol. 214: M. Faber, H. Niemes und G. Stephan, Entropie, Umweltschutz und Rohstoffverbrauch. IX, 181 Seiten. 1983.

Vol. 215: Semi-Infinite Programming and Applications. Proceedings, 1981. Edited by A.V. Fiacco and K.O. Kortanek. XI, 322 pages. 1983.

Vol. 216: H.H. Müller, Fiscal Policies in a General Equilibrium Model with Persistent Unemployment. VI, 92 pages. 1983.

Vol. 217: Ch. Grootaert, The Relation Between Final Demand and Income Distribution. XIV, 105 pages. 1983.

Vol 218: P. van Loon, A Dynamic Theory of the Firm: Production, Finance and Investment. VII, 191 pages. 1983.

Vol. 219: E. van Damme, Refinements of the Nash Equilibrium Concept. VI. 151 pages. 1983.

Vol. 220: M. Aoki, Notes on Economic Time Series Analysis: System Theoretic Perspectives. IX, 249 pages. 1983.

Vol. 221: S. Nakamura, An Inter-Industry Translog Model of Prices and Technical Change for the West German Economy. XIV, 290 pages. 1984.

Vol. 222: P. Meier, Energy Systems Analysis for Developing Countries. VI, 344 pages. 1984.

Vol. 223: W. Trockel, Market Demand. VIII, 205 pages. 1984.

Vol. 224: M. Kiy, Ein disaggregiertes Prognosesystem fur die Bundesrepublik Deutschland. XVIII, 276 Seiten. 1984.

Vol. 225: T.R. von Ungern-Sternberg, Zur Analyse von Märkten mit unvollständiger Nachfragerinformaton. IX, 125 Seiten. 1984.

Vol. 226: Selected Topics in Operations Research and Mathematical Economics. Proceedings, 1963. Edited by G. Hammer and D. Pallaschke IX, 478 pages. 1984.

Vol. 227: Risk and Capital. Proceedings, 1983. Edited by G. Bamberg and K. Spremann VII, 306 pages. 1984.

Vol. 228: Nonlinear Models of Fluctuating Growth. Proceedings, 1983. Edited by R.M. Goodwin, M. Krüger and A. Vercelli. XVII, 277 pages. 1984.

Vol. 229: Interactive Decision Analysis. Proceedings, 1983. Edited by M. Grauer and A.P. Wierzbicki. VIII, 269 pages. 1984.

Vol. 230: Macro-Economic Planning with Conflicting Goals. Proceedings, 1982. Edited by M. Despontin, P. Nijkamp and J. Spronk. VI, 297 pages. 1984.

Vol. 231: G.F. Newell, The M/M/8 Service System with Ranked Servers in Heavy Traffic. XI, 126 pages. 1984.

Vol. 232: L. Bauwens, Bayesian Full Information Analysis of Simultaneous Equation Models Using Integration by Monte Carlo. VI, 114 pages. 1984.

Vol. 233: G. Wagenhals, The World Copper Market. XI, 190 pages. 1984.

Vol. 234: B.C. Eaves, A Course in Triangulations for Solving Equations with Deformations. III, 302 pages. 1984.

Vol. 235: Stochastic Models in Reliability Theory Proceedings, 1984. Edited by S. Osaki and Y. Hatoyama. VII, 212 pages. 1984.

Vol. 236: G. Gandolfo, P.C. Padoan, A Disequilibrium Model of Real and Financial Accumulation in an Open Economy. VI, 172 pages. 1984.

Vol. 237: Misspecification Analysis. Proceedings, 1983. Edited by T.K. Dijkstra. V, 129 pages. 1984.

Vol. 238: W. Domschke, A. Drexl, Location and Layout Planning. IV, 134 pages. 1985.

Vol. 239: Microeconomic Models of Housing Markets. Edited by K. Stahl. VII, 197 pages. 1985.

Vol. 240: Contributions to Operations Research. Proceedings, 1984. Edited by K. Neumann and D. Pallaschke. V, 190 pages. 1985.

Vol. 241: U. Wittmann, Das Konzept rationaler Preiserwartungen. XI, 310 Seiten. 1985.

Vol. 242: Decision Making with Multiple Objectives. Proceedings, 1984. Edited by Y.Y. Haimes and V. Chankong. XI, 571 pages. 1985.

Vol. 243: Integer Programming and Related Areas. A Classified Bibliography 1981–1984. Edited by R. von Randow. XX, 386 pages. 1985.

Vol. 244: Advances in Equilibrium Theory. Proceedings, 1984. Edited by C.D. Aliprantis, O. Burkinshaw and N.J. Rothman. II, 235 pages. 1985.

Vol. 245: J.E.M. Wilhelm, Arbitrage Theory. VII, 114 pages. 1985.

Vol. 246: P.W. Otter, Dynamic Feature Space Modelling, Filtering and Self-Tuning Control of Stochastic Systems. XIV, 177 pages.1985.

Vol. 247: Optimization and Discrete Choice in Urban Systems. Proceedings, 1983. Edited by B.G. Hutchinson, P. Nijkamp and M. Batty Vl, 371 pages. 1985.

Vol. 248: Pural Rationality and Interactive Decision Processes. Proceedings, 1984. Edited by M. Grauer, M. Thompson and A.P. Wierzbicki. VI, 354 pages. 1985.

Vol. 249: Spatial Price Equilibrium: Advances in Theory, Computation and Application. Proceedings, 1984. Edited by P.T. Harker. VII, 277 pages. 1985.

Vol. 250: M. Roubens, Ph. Vincke, Preference Modelling. VIII, 94 pages. 1985.

Vol. 251: Input-Output Modeling. Proceedings, 1984. Edited by A. Smyshlyaev. VI, 261 pages. 1985.

Vol. 252: A. Birolini, On the Use of Stochastic Processes in Modeling Reliability Problems. VI, 105 pages. 1985.

Vol. 253: C. Withagen, Economic Theory and International Trade in Natural Exhaustible Resources. VI, 172 pages. 1985.

Vol. 254: S. Müller, Arbitrage Pricing of Contingent Claims. VIII, 151 pages. 1985.

Vol. 255: Nondifferentiable Optimization: Motivations and Applications. Proceedings, 1984. Edited by V.F. Demyanov and D. Pallaschke. VI, 350 pages. 1985.

Vol. 256: Convexity and Duality in Optimization. Proceedings, 1984. Edited by J. Ponstein. V, 142 pages. 1985.

Vol. 257: Dynamics of Macrosystems. Proceedings, 1984. Edited by J.-P. Aubin, D. Saari and K. Sigmund. VI, 280 pages. 1985.

Vol. 258: H. Funke, Eine allgemeine Theorie der Polypol- und Oligopolpreisbildung. III, 237 pages. 1985.

Vol. 259: Infinite Programming. Proceedings, 1984. Edited by E.J. Anderson and A.B. Philpott. XIV, 244 pages. 1985.

Vol. 260: H.-J. Kruse, Degeneracy Graphs and the Neighbourhood Problem. VIII, 128 pages. 1986.

Vol. 261: Th.R. Gulledge, Jr., N.K. Womer, The Economics of Made-to-Order Production. VI, 134 pages. 1986.

Vol. 262: H.U. Buhl, A Neo-Classical Theory of Distribution and Wealth. V, 146 pages. 1986.

Vol. 263: M. Schäfer, Resource Extraction and Market Struucture. XI, 154 pages. 1986.

Vol. 264: Models of Economic Dynamics. Proceedings, 1983. Edited by H.F. Sonnenschein. VII, 212 pages. 1986.

Vol. 265: Dynamic Games and Applications in Economics. Edited by T. Basar. IX, 288 pages. 1986.

Vol. 266: Multi-Stage Production Planning and Inventory Control. Edited by S. Axsäter, Ch. Schneeweiss and E. Silver. V, 264 pages.1986.

Vol. 267: R. Bemelmans, The Capacity Aspect of Inventories. IX, 165 pages. 1986.

Vol. 268: V. Firchau, Information Evaluation in Capital Markets. VII, 103 pages. 1986.

Vol. 269: A. Borglin, H. Keiding, Optimality in Infinite Horizon Economies. VI, 180 pages. 1986.

Vol. 270: Technological Change, Employment and Spatial Dynamics. Proceedings, 1985. Edited by P. Nijkamp. VII, 466 pages. 1986.

Vol. 271: C. Hildreth, The Cowles Commission in Chicago, 1939–1955. V, 176 pages. 1986.

Vol. 272: G. Clemenz, Credit Markets with Asymmetric Information. VIII,212 pages. 1986.

Vol. 273: Large-Scale Modelling and Interactive Decision Analysis. Proceedings, 1985. Edited by G. Fandel, M. Grauer, A. Kurzhanski and A.P. Wierzbicki. VII, 363 pages. 1986.

Vol. 274: W.K. Klein Haneveld, Duality in Stochastic Linear and Dynamic Programming. VII, 295 pages. 1986.

Vol. 275: Competition, Instability, and Nonlinear Cycles. Proceedings, 1985. Edited by W. Semmler. XII, 340 pages. 1986.

Vol. 276: M.R. Baye, D.A. Black, Consumer Behavior, Cost of Living Measures, and the Income Tax. VII, 119 pages. 1986.

Vol. 277: Studies in Austrian Capital Theory, Investment and Time. Edited by M. Faber. VI, 317 pages. 1986.

Vol. 278: W.E. Diewert, The Measurement of the Economic Benefits of Infrastructure Services. V, 202 pages. 1986.

Vol. 279: H.-J. Büttler, G. Frei and B. Schips, Estimation of Disequilibrium Modes. VI, 114 pages. 1986.

Vol. 280: H.T. Lau, Combinatorial Heuristic Algorithms with FORTRAN. VII, 126 pages. 1986.

Vol. 281: Ch.-L. Hwang, M.-J. Lin, Group Decision Making under Multiple Criteria. XI, 400 pages. 1987.

Vol. 282: K. Schittkowski, More Test Examples for Nonlinear Programming Codes. V, 261 pages. 1987.

Vol. 283: G. Gabisch, H.-W. Lorenz, Business Cycle Theory. VII, 229 pages. 1987.

Vol. 284: H. Lütkepohl, Forecasting Aggregated Vector ARMA Processes. X, 323 pages. 1987.

Vol. 285: Toward Interactive and Intelligent Decision Support Systems. Volume 1. Proceedings, 1986. Edited by Y. Sawaragi, K. Inoue and H. Nakayama. XII, 445 pages. 1987.

Vol. 286: Toward Interactive and Intelligent Decision Support Systems. Volume 2. Proceedings, 1986. Edited by Y. Sawaragi, K. Inoue and H. Nakayama. XII, 450 pages. 1987.

Vol. 287: Dynamical Systems. Proceedings, 1985. Edited by A.B. Kurzhanski and K. Sigmund. VI, 215 pages. 1987.

Vol. 288: G.D. Rudebusch, The Estimation of Macroeconomic Disequilibrium Models with Regime Classification Information. VII,128 pages. 1987.

Vol. 289: B.R. Meijboom, Planning in Decentralized Firms. X, 168 pages. 1987.

Vol. 290: D.A. Carlson, A. Haurie, Infinite Horizon Optimal Control. XI, 254 pages. 1987.

Vol. 291: N. Takahashi, Design of Adaptive Organizations. VI, 140 pages. 1987.

Vol. 292: I. Tchijov, L. Tomaszewicz (Eds.), Input-Output Modeling. Proceedings, 1985. VI, 195 pages. 1987.

Vol. 293: D. Batten, J. Casti, B. Johansson (Eds.), Economic Evolution and Structural Adjustment. Proceedings, 1985. VI, 382 pages.

Vol. 294: J. Jahn, W. Knabs (Eds.), Recent Advances and Historical Development of Vector Optimization. VII, 405 pages. 1987.

Vol. 295. H. Meister, The Purification Problem for Constrained Games with Incomplete Information. X, 127 pages. 1987.

Vol. 296: A. Börsch-Supan, Econometric Analysis of Discrete Choice. VIII, 211 pages. 1987.

Vol. 297: V. Fedorov, H. Läuter (Eds.), Model-Oriented Data Analysis. Proceedings, 1987. VI, 239 pages. 1988.

Vol. 298: S.H. Chew, Q. Zheng, Integral Global Optimization. VII, 179 pages. 1988.

Vol. 299: K. Marti, Descent Directions and Efficient Solutions in Discretely Distributed Stochastic Programs. XIV, 178 pages. 1988.

Vol. 300: U. Derigs, Programming in Networks and Graphs. XI, 315 pages. 1988.

Vol. 301: J. Kacprzyk, M. Roubens (Eds.), Non-Conventional Preference Relations in Decision Making. VII, 155 pages. 1988.

Vol. 302: H.A. Eiselt, G. Pederzoli (Eds.), Advances in Optimization and Control. Proceedings, 1986. VIII, 372 pages. 1988.

Vol. 303: F.X. Diebold, Empirical Modeling of Exchange Rate Dynamics. VII, 143 pages. 1988.

Vol. 304: A. Kurzhanski, K. Neumann, D. Pallaschke (Eds.), Optimization, Parallel Processing and Applications. Proceedings, 1987. VI, 292 pages. 1988.

Vol. 305: G.-J.C.Th. van Schijndel, Dynamic Firm and Investor Behaviour under Progressive Personal Taxation. X, 215 pages.1988.

Vol. 306: Ch. Klein, A Static Microeconomic Model of Pure Competition. VIII, 139 pages. 1988.

Vol. 307: T.K. Dijkstra (Ed.), On Model Uncertainty and its Statistical Implications. VII, 138 pages. 1988.

Vol. 308: J.R. Daduna, A. Wren (Eds.), Computer-Aided Transit Scheduling. VIII, 339 pages. 1988.

Vol. 309: G. Ricci, K. Velupillai (Eds.), Growth Cycles and Multisectoral Economics: the Goodwin Tradition. III, 126 pages. 1988.

Vol. 310: J. Kacprzyk, M. Fedrizzi (Eds.), Combining Fuzzy Imprecision with Probabilistic Uncertainty in Decision Making. IX, 399 pages. 1988.

Vol. 311: R. Färe, Fundamentals of Production Theory. IX, 163 pages. 1988.

Vol. 312: J. Krishnakumar, Estimation of Simultaneous Equation Models with Error Components Structure. X, 357 pages. 1988.

Vol. 313: W. Jammernegg, Sequential Binary Investment Decisions. VI, 156 pages. 1988.

Vol. 314: R. Tietz, W. Albers, R. Selten (Eds.), Bounded Rational Behavior in Experimental Games and Markets. VI, 368 pages. 1988.

Vol. 315: I. Orishimo, G.J.D. Hewings, P. Nijkamp (Eds), Information Technology: Social and Spatial Perspectives. Proceedings 1986. VI, 268 pages. 1988.

Vol. 316: R.L. Basmann, D.J. Slottje, K. Hayes, J.D. Johnson, D.J. Molina, The Generalized Fechner-Thurstone Direct Utility Function and Some of its Uses. VIII, 159 pages. 1988.

Vol. 317: L. Bianco, A. La Bella (Eds.), Freight Transport Planning and Logistics. Proceedings, 1987. X, 568 pages. 1988.

Vol. 318: T. Doup, Simplicial Algorithms on the Simplotope. VIII, 262 pages. 1988.

Vol. 319: D.T. Luc, Theory of Vector Optimization. VIII, 173 pages. 1989.

Vol. 320: D. van der Wijst, Financial Structure in Small Business. VII, 181 pages. 1989.

Vol. 321: M. Di Matteo, R.M. Goodwin, A. Vercelli (Eds.), Technological and Social Factors in Long Term Fluctuations. Proceedings. IX, 442 pages. 1989.

Vol. 322: T. Kollintzas (Ed.), The Rational Expectations Equilibrium Inventory Model. XI, 269 pages. 1989.

Vol. 323: M.B.M. de Koster, Capacity Oriented Analysis and Design of Production Systems. XII, 245 pages. 1989.

Vol. 324: I.M. Bomze, B.M. Pötscher, Game Theoretical Foundations of Evolutionary Stability. VI, 145 pages. 1989.

bor Market and Business

ories of Output, Unem-
1960–1985. XIII, 206

cture and International

Solutions for Strategic

ves, and Taxation. VI,

Investment Policies of
es. 1989.

icki (Eds.), Aspiration
) pages. 1989.

l (Eds.), Cost Analysis
perations Research.

Vol. 333: N. Dellaert, Production to Order. VII, 158 pages. 1989.

Vol. 334: H.-W. Lorenz, Nonlinear Dynamical Economics and Chaotic Motion. XI, 248 pages. 1989.

Vol. 335: A.G. Lockett, G. Islei (Eds.), Improving Decision Making in Organisations. Proceedings. IX, 606 pages. 1989.

Vol. 336: T. Puu, Nonlinear Economic Dynamics. VII, 119 pages. 1989.

Vol. 337: A. Lewandowski, I. Stanchev (Eds.), Methodology and Software for Interactive Decision Support. VIII, 309 pages. 1989.

Vol. 338: J.K. Ho, R.P. Sundarraj, DECOMP: an Implementation of Dantzig-Wolfe Decomposition for Linear Programming. VI, 206 pages.

Vol. 339: J. Terceiro Lomba, Estimation of Dynamic Econometric Models with Errors in Variables. VIII, 116 pages. 1990.

Vol. 340: T. Vasko, R. Ayres, L. Fontvieille (Eds.), Life Cycles and Long Waves. XIV, 293 pages. 1990.

Vol. 341: G.R. Uhlich, Descriptive Theories of Bargaining. IX, 165 pages. 1990.

Vol. 342: K. Okuguchi, F. Szidarovszky, The Theory of Oligopoly with Multi-Product Firms. V, 167 pages. 1990.

Vol. 343: C. Chiarella, The Elements of a Nonlinear Theory of Economic Dynamics. IX, 149 pages. 1990.

Vol. 344: K. Neumann, Stochastic Project Networks. XI, 237 pages. 1990.

Vol. 345: A. Cambini, E. Castagnoli, L. Martein, P Mazzoleni, S. Schaible (Eds.), Generalized Convexity and Fractional Programming with Economic Applications. Proceedings, 1988. VII, 361 pages. 1990.

Vol. 346: R. von Randow (Ed.), Integer Programming and Related Areas. A Classified Bibliography 1984–1987. XIII, 514 pages. 1990.

Vol. 347: D. Ríos Insua, Sensitivity Analysis in Multi-objective Decision Making. XI, 193 pages. 1990.

Vol. 348: H. Störmer, Binary Functions and their Applications. VIII, 151 pages. 1990.

Vol. 349: G.A. Pfann, Dynamic Modelling of Stochastic Demand for Manufacturing Employment. VI, 158 pages. 1990.

Vol. 350: W.-B. Zhang, Economic Dynamics. X, 232 pages. 1990.

Vol. 351: A. Lewandowski, V. Volkovich (Eds.), Multiobjective Problems of Mathematical Programming. Proceedings, 1988. VII, 315 pages. 1991.

Vol. 352: O. van Hilten, Optimal Firm Behaviour in the Context of Technological Progress and a Business Cycle. XII, 229 pages. 1991.

Vol. 353: G. Ricci (Ed.), Decision Processes in Economics. Proceedings, 1989. III, 209 pages 1991.

Vol. 354: M. Ivaldi, A Structural Analysis of Expectation Formation. XII, 230 pages. 1991.

Vol. 355: M. Salomon. Deterministic Lotsizing Models for Production Planning. VII, 158 pages. 1991.

Vol. 356: P. Korhonen, A. Lewandowski, J . Wallenius (Eds.), Multiple Criteria Decision Support. Proceedings, 1989. XII, 393 pages. 1991.

Vol. 357: P. Zörnig, Degeneracy Graphs and Simplex Cycling. XV, 194 pages. 1991.

Vol. 358: P. Knottnerus, Linear Models with Correlated Disturbances. VIII, 196 pages. 1991.

Vol. 359: E. de Jong, Exchange Rate Determination and Optimal Economic Policy Under Various Exchange Rate Regimes. VII, 270 pages. 1991.

Vol. 360: P. Stalder, Regime Translations, Spillovers and Buffer Stocks. VI, 193 pages . 1991.

Vol. 361: C. F. Daganzo, Logistics Systems Analysis. X, 321 pages. 1991.

Vol. 362: F. Gehrels, Essays In Macroeconomics of an Open Economy. VII, 183 pages. 1991.

Vol. 363: C. Puppe, Distorted Probabilities and Choice under Risk. VIII, 100 pages . 1991

Vol. 364: B. Horvath, Are Policy Variables Exogenous? XII, 162 pages. 1991.

Vol. 365: G. A. Heuer, U. Leopold-Wildburger. Balanced Silverman Games on General Discrete Sets. V, 140 pages. 1991.

Vol. 366: J. Gruber (Ed.), Econometric Decision Models. Proceedings, 1989. VIII, 636 pages. 1991.

Vol. 367: M. Grauer, D. B. Pressmar (Eds.), Parallel Computing and Mathematical Optimization. Proceedings. V, 208 pages. 1991.

Vol. 368: M. Fedrizzi, J. Kacprzyk, M. Roubens (Eds.), Interactive Fuzzy Optimization. VII, 216 pages. 1991.

Vol. 369: R. Koblo, The Visible Hand. VIII, 131 pages.1991.

Vol. 370: M. J. Beckmann, M. N. Gopalan, R. Subramanian (Eds.), Stochastic Processes and their Applications. Proceedings, 1990. XLI, 292 pages. 1991.

Vol. 371: A. Schmutzler, Flexibility and Adjustment to Information in Sequential Decision Problems. VIII, 198 pages. 1991.

Vol. 372: J. Esteban, The Social Viability of Money. X, 202 pages. 1991.

Vol. 373: A. Billot, Economic Theory of Fuzzy Equilibria. XIII, 164 pages. 1992.

Vol. 374: G. Pflug, U. Dieter (Eds.), Simulation and Optimization. Proceedings, 1990. X, 162 pages. 1992.

Vol. 375: S.-J. Chen, Ch.-L. Hwang, Fuzzy Multiple Attribute Decision Making. XII, 536 pages. 1992.

Vol. 376: K.-H. Jöckel, G. Rothe, W. Sendler (Eds.), Bootstrapping and Related Techniques. Proceedings, 1990. VIII, 247 pages. 1992.

Vol. 377: A. Villar, Operator Theorems with Applications to Distributive Problems and Equilibrium Models. XVI, 160 pages. 1992.

Vol. 378: W. Krabs, J. Zowe (Eds.), Modern Methods of Optimization. Proceedings, 1990. VIII, 348 pages. 1992.

Vol. 379: K. Marti (Ed.), Stochastic Optimization. Proceedings, 1990. VII, 182 pages. 1992.

Vol. 380: J. Odelstad, Invariance and Structural Dependence. XII, 245 pages. 1992.

Vol. 381: C. Giannini, Topics in Structural VAR Econometrics. XI, 131 pages. 1992.